A HISTORY
OF
ROCESTER

Alan Gibson

ACKNOWLEDGEMENTS

Lichfield Records Office.
Stafford Records Office.
Stoke on Trent Records Office.
Lichfield Library.
Hanley Library.
Uttoxeter Library.
Birmingham University. Ian Ferris.
Hanley Museum.
W. Hirst. J. Palmer. Mrs. D. Bond. JCB Records.
G. Egerton. St. Michael P. C. C.
P. Harrison.
S. Glover.
K. Langton.
B. Davies.
J. Capper.
Mrs M. Clarke.
Derek Sederman. Abbotsholme School.

My thank to Ms Sue Harrison who has once again made sense out of my
writing and transferred it to the word processor for me.

Other books by Alan Gibson

History of Doveridge
Millennium Doveridge
Bittersweet: Memories of Cheddleton
Staffordshire Legends

Roman picture cover courtesy of Mark Olly, from his series of books on
Warrington antiquities, *CELTIC WARRINGTON & OTHER MYSTERIES, VOLS I, II &III*

CHURNET VALLEY BOOKS
1 King Street, Leek, Staffordshire. ST13 5NW   01538 399033
thebookshopleek.co.uk
© Alan Gibson and Churnet Valley Books 2003
ISBN 1 897949 95 2

Printed and bound by Bath Press

CONTENTS

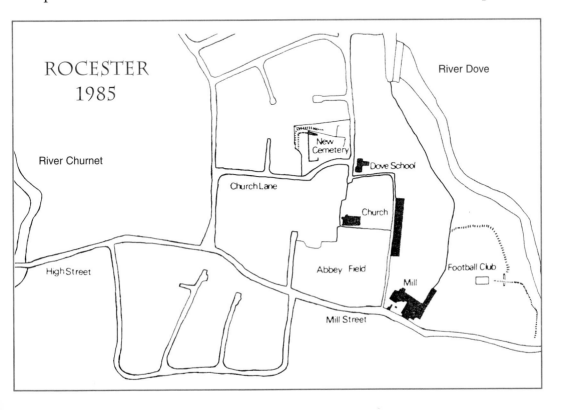

ROCESTER TOWNSHIP

The bric-a-brac of history
lies beneath the feet
of the ghosts of Roman soldiers
walking Rocester streets.

The wares of ancient nations
buried deep within the clay
bear witness to the stories
and the tales of yesterday.

And the echo's of past glories
are narrated by the sage,
to wide eyed village children
who cannot read the page.

He tells of Norman conquest
of monastery and church
of Henrys dissolution and
the church of Rome's reverse

Then Industrial Revolution
is welcomed with a will
as Arkwright comes from Cromford
to build a cotton mill

And the seeds of education
fall on fertile ground
where it mixes with ambition
where the working man abounds.

And the tides of evolution
that even out life's span
bring equal opportunity
to the brotherhood of man.

'Ornamented Celt' from Redfern's *History of Uttoxeter*.

ONE
PRE-ROMAN AND ROMAN ROCESTER

Long before our Anglo-Saxon forebears divided the nation into shires, and the shires into hundreds, the land was inhabited by the Neolithic pioneers who settled into the area with no worries about taxation or county boundaries. The land we now conveniently think of as West Derbyshire and East Staffordshire was as attractive then as it is now. The River Dove and the River Churnet carved their way through wild untamed terrain before reaching the broad valleys left by an earlier ice age. These broad valleys were now fertile and lush. From the west they were joined by the River Trent, equally attractive to Neolithic man. The great forest of Lyme held good bounty, including deer and boar; rivers teemed with fish and meadow lands were packed with edible berries and roots. Those nomadic hunters who finally chose to settle here, could hardly have picked a better spot. Along the banks of the Dove, and in the valley of the Trent, permanent settlements were formed and evidence of their existence remains today.

The Trent valley, particularly rich in artefacts, culminates in a settlement at Trent Vale. Flint tools, arrow heads and the bric-a-brac of Neolithic life abound. Closer to our village are objects discovered during the 20th century. In 1934, Albert Fradley, working at Cubley Carr, found part of a damaged stone adze. In far better condition was a polished stone axe found by Mr G. Cope at Woodhouse Farm. The axe, described as siltstone, was discovered about one hundred yards from Brocksford Brook (SK 129 352) and measured $5^{1}/_{2}$" x $2^{1}/_{2}$" x $1^{1}/_{2}$".

Of a later age, two bronze implements were found at Somersal Herbert. The palistave and the flanged axe were unearthed in about 1850. In the village of Rocester itself, a Bronze Age decorated pot was discovered in Northfield Avenue during routine road repairs. At Barrow Hill, to the north of Rocester, a small Iron Age hill fort existed and, to the south of the village, several barrows indicate the burial grounds of a settled community.

Ancient flints found in the area

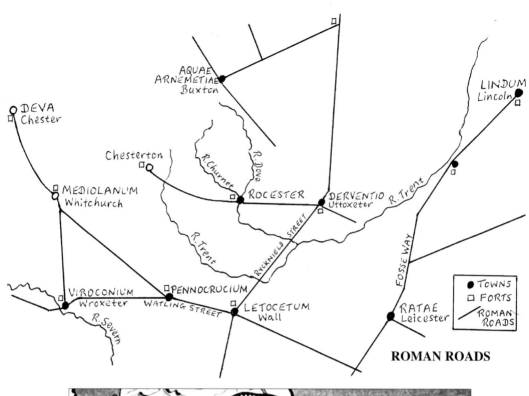

ROMAN ROADS

Of even greater significance are the artefacts found during excavations on the site of a Roman fort at Rocester. Whilst not a major settlement, it has provided a rare mix of household goods, tools and personal relics, and mixed into this pot-pourri of the Roman period are the remains of the Abbey of St. Mary, built on the site of the Roman fort in the middle of the 12th century.

Gaius Julius Caesar had achieved his ambition - Gaul was under the control of Rome and he now contemplated the invasion of Britain. The island had long harboured refugees from Germany and Gaul, among whom were many die hards who refused to bow to Rome. His intelligence services told of a warrior race, of Druids and half civilised savages, who appeased their gods with human sacrifices. But such a reputation did little to deter Caesar and, in the Roman year 699 (55 BC), he gathered together eighty units of transport, two legions of the Roman army and set sail for the coast of Britain.

The story of the courage of the Roman standard bearer and the bloody battle that followed has secured its place in history. In reality Caesar's invasion was short-lived and, although he returned in triumph to Rome, Britain was far from vanquished. Caesar had the misfortune to come up against Cassivellaunus, a leader who can justifiably be called our first British hero. It was Cassivellaunus who, as leader of the warrior Druids, caused Caesar his greatest problems.

Over a distance of several miles the British fought for their lives. The skill and daring of the charioteers was sufficient to cut swathes of devastation through the Roman army. Despite the mayhem and the heavy losses the invaders stood firm. As the Romans gained ground it was a wise Cassivellaunus who recognised the limitations of his followers. Under a truce he negotiated peace terms with Caesar which allowed the Roman leader to return home in triumph with Cassivellaunus as his hostage, and Britain, technically under the heel of Rome, continued life exactly as they had before.

For the best part of a hundred years the only contact between Britain and Rome lay in the hands of merchants. Where the armies had failed, commerce succeeded and, whilst subjugation was not on the agenda, the ways of the island race became much better known.

In AD 41, the Emperor Caligula met an untimely death and, after much bitterness and dispute he was replaced by Claudius. Claudius, supposedly a scholar, was volatile to the point of madness. Death was available at a whim. Those in favour one day could face execution the next. Wiser councillors tried to harness his energies in ways that were politic to their own ambition. To these councillors, the stories of a Britain where trade flourished and natural wealth abounded, not only bore the hallmark of truth, but presented great opportunity to gain favour with Claudius.

The suggestion of an invasion struck a chord with Claudius and, in AD 43 a vast well organised army once again prepared to invade Britain. Under the control of Plautius, the Romans landed once more on British soil. There was to be no turning back. The British leader Caractacus, and his brother Togodumanus fought

The Romans arriving in 55 BC and fighting the British.

(drawings from Celtic Warrington & Other Mysteries by Mark Olly)

much in the style of Cassivellaunus, with a combination of guerrilla attacks and chariot led forays. The Romans pressed ahead, driving the British deep into the countryside. The turning point came about twelve miles inland. Reaching a river we now know as the Medway the British made their stand.

Superior local knowledge enabled the British to place the river between themselves and the Romans, and Caractacus and his followers waited for the Romans to attempt the deep flowing river. Vespasion, a Roman general, allowed his forces to rest whilst he devised a strategy. As dusk approached Vespasion despatched a detachment of Germans to a point up river where, despite their heavy armour, they were able to cross. Instead of attacking the British flank the Germans swiftly disabled the horses. The use of chariots was impossible now and in the confusion that followed the Romans crossed en-masse.

Two days of bitter fighting followed before Vespasion emerged victorious. But for Plautius the battle was over too quickly - Claudius had had designs on a Roman victory for himself. Such was his ego and eccentricity that he arrived from Gaul with reinforcements. Another battle was conveniently arranged which the Romans won and Claudius, with a great victory under his belt, returned in triumph to Rome and the senate.

Britain may have been conquered but it was far from beaten. Many tribal races existed in Britain and each and every one did its utmost to deter the Roman advance. The Roman governor was kept in a constant state of alert. The King of the Iceni was killed in battle, but in his wake arose his wife, a furious Boadicea. Gathering the Iceni and anyone else who would follow, Boadicea attacked while the main Roman army was occupied in Wales, and routed the Roman army in the south. Marching on, she took the city of Colchester and then London. Huge reinforcements, in the form of a complete legion, were required before the Romans could defeat Boadicea's army.

The Romans now decided a more robust and sustainable course of action was required. A new governor, Agricola, was appointed in AD 78. Agricola saw no point in conquest if it was followed by constant war. He opted for a firm but conciliatory path. Law Courts were established, temples and administrative centres erected, roads were laid and garrisons built at intervals along the routes. British leaders were educated in the ways of Rome and the old hierarchy found a place in the new order. A degree of indulgence and a recognition of human weakness kept the British under control.

From the Roman centre of Littlechester (Derby) the road headed west towards Chesterton (Newcastle) and beyond. Midway between the two a protective fort was built. In the flat lands, before the River Dove and the River Churnet join forces, the Roman village of Rocester was born. The fort, with its detachment of soldiers, its clerics and civilians was to quickly establish itself.

Between AD 78 and AD 88 the township grew to prominence. Trade flourished, local tradesmen plied their crafts, and visitors sold their wares. Agriculture met the challenge of greater demand, the Romans themselves setting standards of excellence hitherto unknown. The story for us of the Roman presence at Rocester could well have ended at that point. The fact that the story continues owes much to local historians and, more recently, to the dedication of the field archaeology unit of Birmingham University.

With the financial support of Sir Anthony Bamford of JCB Excavators and the expertise of individuals such as Ian Ferris, Dr Graham Webster, Fiona Chapman-Purchase and Malcolm Cooper, plus a work force often unheralded but much appreciated, a more detailed picture of life emerges.

Excavations had taken place in and around Rocester for many years. Redfern's *History of Uttoxeter* records the discovery of Roman artefacts; finds are recorded in 1792, 1833, 1835, 1852 and 1888. Between 1913 and 1960/62 several trenches were dug, one across the playing fields of the Dove First School (Barns 1914), and in 1958-59 members of the Oldfield Boys School dug a number of trenches to the north of Church Lane and in Abbey Field. Their remarkable discoveries deserve far greater praise than they received.

A sewage trench was dug across Abbey Field in 1960/62 and, although the presence of stone work was recorded, it was thought to relate to the medieval abbey rather than the Roman fort. Unfortunately, a less than thorough analysis of the artefacts uncovered led to frustration for the more professional archaeologists that followed.

In 1961 Dr Graham Webster, alerted by the proximity of the Littlechester to Chesterton Roman Road, the main alignment of which crosses the Dove to the south of the village, by the cester place name, and by the discoveries of Roman materials, visited Rocester. Webster noted an earthwork on the boundary of the New Cemetery. Its curving site suggested to him that it might be the corner of a Roman Fort. A trial trench proved his hypothesis to be correct. The results were a revelation:

1. A late first-century earthen rampart inside which was a series of trenches for the sleeper beams of timber buildings. These were interpreted as a part of a Roman fort.
2. Sometime after AD 160 a second rampart was built along the line of the original rampart. It was suggested that this might form part of the defences of a civil settlement.
3. Part of this second bank was cut away to allow the insertion of a stone wall, contemporary with which was a quarry pit of AD 280 or later.
4. This pit was overlain by a tilling layer containing fourth century pottery.
5. This was in turn overlain by a marked horizon of burning, which yielded a late Saxon strap end dated to the late ninth century, and also a number of knife blades.
6. In the medieval period the area was used for dumping of quantities of stone rubble.

Without detracting from the efforts of earlier enthusiasts it is apparent that Dr Webster was the first professional to carry out a proper archaeological dig on the Rocester site. His findings are even more remarkable given the restrictions imposed by a cemetery which had already been in use for over ten years before his excavation. The New Cemetery will no doubt make future digs more and more difficult, perhaps making a final conclusion impossible.

At this point we should consider the enigma of the second rampart that was built around 160 AD. If, as is widely suggested, the Romans entered into a period of regional demilitarisation and the fort at Rocester was abandoned, why would it be necessary to rebuild the rampart? Evidence from excavations also point to a levelling of ramparts and a dismantling of buildings. One answer to the puzzle could be that the fort was not abandoned entirely but simply reduced in number and size. With a token force of soldiers the civilian population would have felt it essential to improve the defensive ramparts of what was fast becoming an important township.

In 1985, under the guidance of Ian Ferris* and Malcolm Cooper, of Birmingham University, further excavations were carried out. The excavation lasted thirteen weeks from the 6th May to 2nd August when a 30 metre by 10 metre area was

* Ian Ferris is director of the Birmingham University Field Archaeology Unit. His precis *Rocester Excavation Project 1986* provides much of the information used in the preceding pages. Ian's publication and a detailed catalogue of artefacts and excavation details are held in the records section of Uttoxeter library. My thanks to Ian Ferris for his co-operation.

opened in the New Cemetery. Dr. Webster's trench was also re-opened. The objective was to provide an archaeological sequence, to discover and date artefacts within a related time span and to expand upon knowledge from previous digs.

Again remarkable results were achieved. The work of Ferris and Cooper produced a far wider and more diverse cross section of material than could have been anticipated. Cobbled sections, large pots, a beam trench and floor surfaces all relate to the Roman period. Pottery shards in large quantities ranged from Roman times through to the13th and 14th century. Four spits contained large amounts of residual Roman pottery.

Occasional ploughing and the layering of foreign deposits cause uncertainty in some areas, but all the activity leads to the conclusion that Rocester was a thriving community both during and after the Roman occupation. Over the whole site the evidence is for an end to cultivation in the late 18th century. This would coincide very well with the industrial revolution and the introduction of the Rocester Mill on the banks of the Dove.

The sheer volume of objects uncovered by Ferris and Cooper is staggering: One hundred and eleven copper alloy objects, including thirty-one Roman coins. One thousand five hundred nails and two hundred iron objects. Four thousand shards of pottery of Roman manufacture, one thousand of medieval date and two thousand post-medieval. Included in the pottery were Staffordshire and Derbyshire ware. From further afield come fine wares from the Nene Valley, North Warwickshire and Oxford. Also present was Black Burnished ware from Dorset, Samian ware, possibly from central Gaul, and fragments of Amphora from Spain. Much of the pottery dated from the first century to the fourth century and was in accord with the dates of the coins. The discoveries indicate more and more the scope of trade and commerce undertaken at Rocester.

It would appear, from the archaeological discoveries that Rocester, with its wooden barracks, military personnel and civilian population, may well have been the most important township in the area. It almost certainly surpassed Uttoxeter at the time. Ian Ferris gives an estimated population of around 1,200 people during the main period of Roman activity.

It would also appear that far from declining after the Romans departed, Rocester continued as a busy trading centre. The artefacts, especially the pottery, indicate continued occupation and although little is known about pre-Norman Rocester, post Roman discoveries support the theory that the community went on. A strap end from the Webster excavation is dated as 9th century and the Staffordshire ware discovered in 1986 is of the 10th century.

We know that in the post-Roman turmoil the Kingdom of Mercia emerged. The five hundred year gap in our knowledge leaves us wondering about Rocester in this period, but we can be fairly sure the people were still going about their business much as before.

Roman coins found in Rocester
Claudius II, above, AD 268-270
Tetricus I, below, AD 270-274

A spoon found in Orton's Pasture, Rocester. The bowl is approx. 20 cms diameter

Below: pieces found at Barrow Hill by Francis Redfern which appear in his *History of Uttoxeter* 1863

SAMIAN WARE.

SALOPIAN BOWL.

ROCESTER

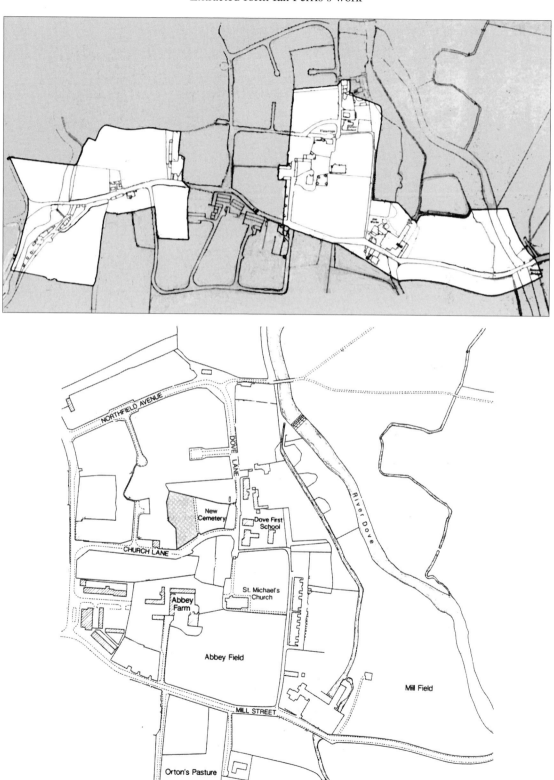

Replica of a Roman gaming board with white pieces found at Trent Vale, and a black piece found at Rocester

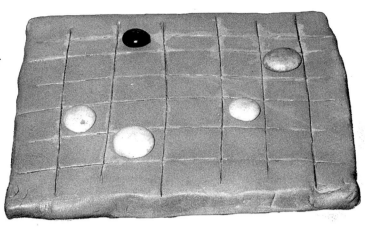

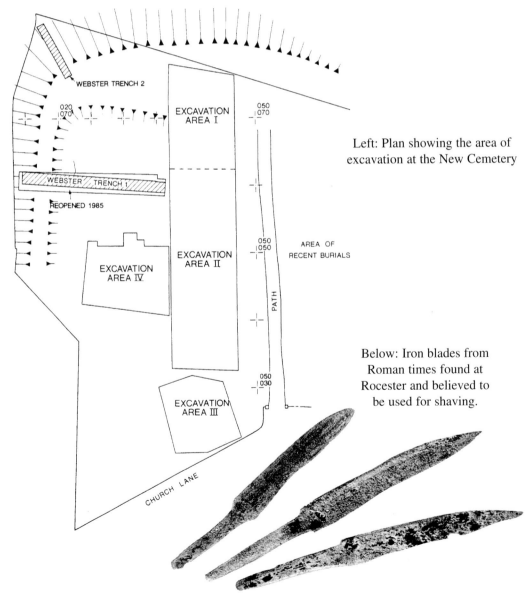

Left: Plan showing the area of excavation at the New Cemetery

Below: Iron blades from Roman times found at Rocester and believed to be used for shaving.

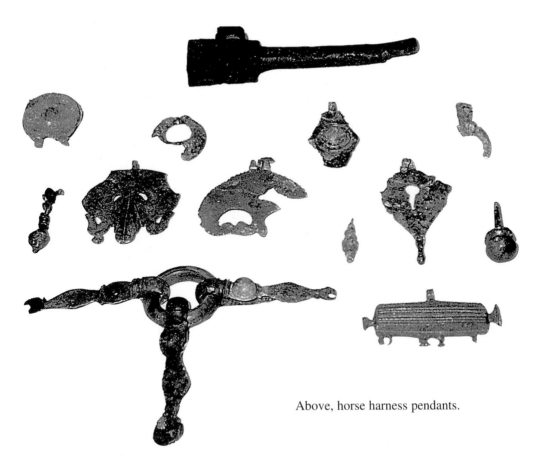

Above, horse harness pendants.

Below armour fragments. All pieces found at Rocester.

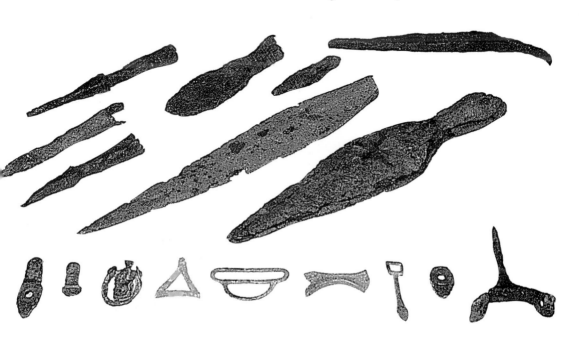

Waves of Germanic immigrants 'anglicised' parts of Britain after the Romans left.

Was there a church in Rocester in Norman times?

TWO
THE POST ROMAN ERA

As the Roman Empire began to crumble, more and more legions were recalled. Britain was left to its own devices, mainly to administrators schooled in the ways of Rome. The Romans were never to return and, as the reality dawned, the power struggle began. If a new order was to be imposed the road to power had to be travelled quickly. The problems lay in the number of people on that road. Old families, tribal leaders, hereditary land owners and the new hierarchy all sought to impose their will on a nation that was leaderless and ripe for the picking.

The battle for supremacy dragged on over decades as the Country descended into what would now be described as civil war. It was to be almost six hundred years before Britain was united under a common cause and a single monarch again. The net result was a land divided into several distinct areas, each with its own king or leader. The lessons of Rome were all but forgotten. In the centre of England the Kingdom of Mercia reigned supreme, both in terms of the growth of Christianity and the fight for overall supremacy.

The *Anglo Saxon Chronicle*, the works of Bede, Gildas and Nennuis, all record the national events and affairs of church and state. The minutiae of everyday Britain with its hamlets and villages are rarely considered worthy of record - if the affairs of Rocester, Uttoxeter and the like merited inclusion the details have yet to be revealed. What we are left with, is the impression of a nation subjected to attack from all and sundry. The Jutes, the Angles, the Saxons, from the Germanic areas of Europe, and the Picts, mainly from Scotland, all sought a share of the spoils. Later, as the millennium approached, the Vikings firmly imposed their will.

Just as the Romans had settled in Britain, so did the Northern European invaders, and the indigenous Briton merged with the invaders. Saxons in particular settled and either took over existing communities or simply set up home alongside the earlier settlers. Saxon names are now an integral part of our language; the Saxon endings 'ton' 'ham' and 'ing' all relating to hamlets or villages. Hollington and Marchington, for example, and tons proliferate: Alton, Denstone, Marston, Foston, Scropton and Boylestone to name but a few. These communities traded locally, and we know from excavations that Rocester and Uttoxeter traded nationally. All in all, life, most of the time,went on as it always had.

Perhaps more important was the growth of Christianity. Often, religious ambitions went hand in hand with national ambition. Paeda, son of King Penda, was converted to Christianity but still had to fight for the survival of his Mercian Kingdom. The influence of Ireland and Scotland on Christianity in Britain is without question and it was from those outposts that the bishops and monks travelled into Mercia in general and to Repton in particular. The early monastic centres provided the impetus for religious learning and from these centres priests travelled to village and town to educate the population, whilst keeping the peace with the lord of the manor, who, often as not, had an equal desire for Christian knowledge. The support of the king, of course, eased their passage.

The villages as we know them were formed. The church, with its priest at the centre of village life, became the norm, and Rocester, despite its fine modern church, would almost certainly have had a Saxon church for the spiritual needs of its citizens.

Despite the success of the early monastic establishments and the changes they brought to English life, their ecclesiastical powers were limited. The king and his earls still held the balance of power. When the Vikings arrived they virtually ransacked the Country. Monasteries and villages were destroyed almost as a matter of principle by a heathen invader who displayed neither sympathy for the people or the church. For a while the Country was in real danger of being overrun, but early in the 11th century, the British rose behind a Saxon king, Aethelred, who demanded that all Vikings should be removed from the land. A fierce battle took place at Hounds Hill near Marchington. Surely the men of Rocester, Eaton, Uttoxeter and Doveridge would have fought in that great battle, and tales of valour and victory would have passed from generation to generation.

The compromise with Danes that Aethelred's victories brought, and the relative peace, lasted but three generations. In 1066 William of Normandy, pursuing what he considered his right to the English throne, arrived with an army at Hastings. He was met by Harold, whose exhausted troops, wearied by recent battles and a long march, fought to the bitter end. England again found itself under foreign rule.

After the conquest Algar was dispossessed of his land and ownership passed to the crown or then the appointees of William. In the case of Rocester we note that much of the village was laid to waste as William imposed his will.

Twenty years on, William was well enough established to take stock of his kingdom, and the *Domesday Book* of 1086 records the details and value of his realm. As is so often the case, we owe thanks to those clerics who completed the survey - we can see clearly there the story of local villages like Rocester, Marston Montgomery, Cubley, Somersal Herbert, Sudbury and Doveridge. The entry for Rocester reads:

Earl Algar held it.
> *1 hide, with its dependencies.*
> *Land for 9 plough. In Lordship 2.*
> *18 Villagers and 10 smallholders with 9 ploughs.*
> *A mill at 10s, meadow 20 acres, woodland 1 furlong and as wide.*
> *Value before 1066 £4, now £8.0.0*

Uttoxeter was of similar size and wealth:

Earl Algar held it.
> *½ hide, land for 10 ploughs.*
> *In Lordship 2, with 1 slave.*
> *24 villagers and 11 smallholders with 11 ploughs.*
> *Meadow 16 acres, woodland 2 leagues long and as wide.*
> *Value before 1066 £7, now £8.0.0*

THREE
THE ABBEY OF ST. MARY

Many of the monasteries that proliferated during the early centuries of the second millennium did so at the whim or largesse of the Lord of the Manor. For a while it became almost the done thing for a house of religion to be established by the rich and powerful. Often, the choice of site or the determination of creed makes little sense although it may well have matched the ideals of the provider. Some monasteries were destined to play an important role in the religious affairs of the nation whilst others, admirable as they may have been, were content to make up the numbers or to drift along in their accustomed role. The role of Rocester as an Augustinian abbey is difficult to define. It was certainly among the smallest and indeed the poorest of abbeys, although its financial returns raise a few questions and give reason to doubt whether it was as poor as it made out.

The abbey of St. Mary was founded between 1141 and 1146 by Richard Bacon, a nephew of Ranulph, Earl of Chester. The foundation charter states that Richard gave to Thurstan, the first Abbot, and to his canons, the church of Rocester together with the Vills of Rocester and East Bridgeford (Notts) and the lands and tenements belonging to them.

A second charter, although of unsure origin, enlarges on the detail of Richard's largesse and states as follows;

Richard gave the canons the church of Rocester with its chapels of Bradley-in-the-moors and Waterfall, the vills of Rocester and Combridge and his demesnes there, and at Wooton with appurtenances and liberties in Nothill (Croxden), Denstone, Quixhill, Roston, Bradley-in-the-moors, Waterfall and Calton; and in East Bridgeford, 8 carucates and 2 bovates of land and to the third part of two mills.

The men of Rocester, Combridge, Nothill, Roston, Waterfall and Bradley were ordered to continue to render the services and suit of court at Rocester which they had rendered successively to Earl Ranulph and to his nephew. Richard's gift was confirmed by Earl Ranulph de Blunderville in about 1200.

Whether or not the second charter is considered genuine the fact remains that J.A. Hibbert in his *Dissolution of Monasteries* (1909) quotes freely from *Valor Ecclesiasticus,* the official documents relating to fiscal practise, and links Rocester with Waterfall and Bradley, and also with Edensor and Woodford, indicating that the second charter was valid and the association of the parishes was recognised by the commissioners at the Dissolution.

In the absence of a plan of the abbey or a precise layout of its lands we are left to build on what little we know. Even the smallest of abbeys would require essentials to meet the demands of its occupants. A church may seem an obvious start. The abbot and the monks needed somewhere to live. The abbots house would have its own garden and kitchens. Dormitories and relaxation areas for the monks, cloisters and herb edged lawns surrounded the church. On one side would be kitchens, a laundry and a store room. There would also be an infirmary, a physician, a chapel and a library; perhaps even a school or a building dedicated to academic study.

On the perimeter of the monastic centre stood the practical requirements of everyday life. Stables, cow sheds, pig stys and outbuildings. A work area would cater for carpenters, masons, smiths, wheelwrights and gardeners, as well as the baker and brewer. A great deal of self-sufficiency was called for from the monastic dweller. The Augustinians were as secular as any in their outlook but still found religious sanctuary a necessity.

Outside the walls of the monastery, the demesne land of the abbey lay between the River Dove and the River Churnet. Additional lands elsewhere contributed to a comfortable, if not prosperous, lifestyle. If we are to judge by the size of the estate after the Dissolution we see that the abbey comprised of:

*The manors of Rocester, Combridge and Quixhill, with 26 messuages, 10 cottages, 40 barns, 38 stables, 35 orchards, 400 acres of arable land, 400 acres of meadow, 800 acres of pasture, 20 acres of woodland, 30 acres of furze and heath, £1-16-00 in rents, common pasture for cattle, common of turbary, courts leet, courts baron, view of frankpledge, franchises, waifs, estrays, good and chattels of felons and fugitives, deeds and escheats, fines and amercements in the above and in Crakemarsh, Prestwood and lands in Alton, Ellastone, Uttoxeter and Checkley. Tithes of corn and hay. Advowson of vicarage of Rocester church. **

Income recorded in the *Valor Ecclesiasticus* amounted to around £100 per annum. No doubt the income was net - ie what was left over - with the needs of the abbey being met from their own farms and workshops. One hundred pounds was a substantial amount of money and even though social and economic changes make a comparison impossible, a figure of between £50,000 and £100,000 in today's terms would not be unreasonable. The monks seemed reluctant to distribute any of their gains to the village churches but only too willing to receive whatever gifts came their way. Details from the *Valor Ecclesiasticus* confirm this reluctance very plainly!

Traditionally, much of the income from the land came from the sale of wool. Pegolotti, carrying out his survey of religious houses in North Staffordshire, visited Rocester and noted that the abbey produced 10 sacks of wool from 2,400 sheep. The largest abbey in Staffordshire, Burton, produced 25 sacks. Also noted was the husbandry of cattle, pigs, hens and geese. It would appear that if the abbey was run efficiently and wisely, any claims of poverty were totally false.

From time to time catastrophes beyond their control would result in temporary setbacks. Drought and floods, famine and fire caused tremendous problems to agriculture. Even worse was the Black Death. The plague occured throughout the life of the abbey and, on occasions, the loss of life was so great that labour became a problem and tithes were lost as tenant farmers failed to work the land. Even so, a wise hand on the fiscal purse procured a reliable income for most of the time. If claims of poverty are to be believed they are more likely to have originated from the periods of lawlessness and abuse of privilege by the abbot and the monks.

In 1229 Bishop Stavensby gave the abbey permission to appropriate the church of Rocester with its chapels and appurtenances. The first hint of 'poverty' is revealed when the charter states that the canons of Rocester suffered greater poverty than any other religious house in the diocese. To ease their poverty they were granted immunity or freedom from all Episcopal custom except for 3s-00 Peters pence. They were also granted the right to serve their parish church by one of their own brethren. Despite the efforts of Bishop Stavensby in 1240-41 the sheriff was ordered to give the canons twelve marks for their clothing and two marks to buy a pipe of wine. They also received further gifts: In 1246 the king gave a silver gilt communion cup and the following year he gave ten marks to the abbey. Some years later, in 1277, a grant of royal protection exempted the abbey from contributing to the costs of the king's army in Wales.

In the 13th century more substantial grants followed in an effort to improve the abbey's financial situation. In 1283 the right to hold a Thursday market at Rocester plus a yearly fair on the feast of St. Edmund during November (15th to 17th) was granted. Help continued over the decades. In 1284 Bishop Neuland granted the canons the right to appropriate Kingston church and shortly afterwards, the rector, Henry of Marchington, assigned to the abbey an annual pension of £2 from the church.

It seems that despite all this largesse the abbey was still poor and burdened with debt through maintaining hospitality for poor travellers. The wealth of the abbey was now given as an income of £28-16-4 per annum. Almost half of this was from the church at Rocester which contributed £13-6-8. The villagers must have wondered from time to time about the depth of their relationship with the monastery, and in 1331 relations reached a low point when the inhabitants complained that they were not receiving sacraments in the parish church of St. Mary as was the custom on Easter day. The canons claimed that such sacraments could be administered at their own conventual church. The Bishop, when called upon to intervene, decided that parishioners might attend either church.

Troubles continued for the canons. Their lives were marked more by quarrels and negligence than by peace and endeavour. One of the canons, probably Geoffrey Spagurnel, was sent to the king's court on business. No doubt intent on a good time, he was accused of retaining documents and spending much of the abbey's money. The same Geoffrey was in trouble again in 1337 for breaking into Bolingbroke Castle, when he and a number of laymen imprisoned Alice, Countess of Lincoln and took away 20 horses. Geoffrey's actions were but a forerunner of things to come.

These acts of lawlessness seem to indicate a cavalier attitude towards common law and an abuse of privilege by those in a position of authority. The abbot and his monks would certainly consider themselves in a position of authority, with their

A drawing of a typical abbey of the time - how Rocester may have looked.

The Seal of Rocester Abbey

Below: The Abbey Fields

substantial demesne and additional lands, plus their rights and privileges. Disputes are recorded frequently and are not limited to one person or one era.

Early in the 13th century Geoffrey de Denstone pleaded that the abbot of Rocester had unjustly dispossessed him of his common pasture at Barrow Hill. The abbot claimed that Northullehay (Barrow Hill) was not a village pasture but a piece of land that was a part of the Rocester pasture. He also claimed that Geoffrey held nothing in the vill of Rocester from which he could claim, but only through his wife, Margaret, who was not named in the writ. Geoffrey withdrew but was too poor to pay his lawyer's fees.

In 1261 the abbot of Rocester sued Robert de Akovir (Okeover) and Margaret, his wife, for entering his wood at Northull and destroying the herbage and pannage. The outcome is unknown although it would indicate that the abbot had established a claim on Northull possibly at the time of the earlier dispute with Geoffrey de Denstone.

The Okeovers were involved, albeit indirectly, in a more serious affair in 1290. Hugh, a miller in the employ of Robert de Okeover, was in an ale house with Agnes, a servant of Robert de Okeover, and Hugh, the son of a carter from Rocester. An argument developed between the men and Hugh from Okeover struck Hugh from Rocester on the head with an iron bar. As a result he died and Hugh the miller fled the scene and was outlawed.

By 1375 perhaps the most notorious of the abbey canons was causing mayhem with his misdeeds in and around Rocester. Richard de Foston was a canon of the monastery during the time of the abbots Thomas of Rocester (1364-1375) and John Cheswardine (1375-1386). Foston seems to have been something of a wastrel who wandered the countryside in secular attire. He was arrested for his deeds, in 1375, by William de Verney of Denstone, John Basset (Sheriff of Staffordshire), William de Haughton and Thomas de Stafford. Whatever he had done merited the action of four senior figures.

Not that those in authority over him were without fault. William de Verney had been implicated in the murders of William de Grenburgh in 1361 and Hugh Coyney in 1373. The murder of Coyney may well have resulted from an earlier quarrel when he sued de Verney for taking by force of arms a boar and sixteen pigs worth ten marks from Alveton, plus chattels and goods worth 40 shillings.

In 1375 Rocester appointed a new abbot from outside the monastery. John Cheswardine was a canon from Ranton Priory and by all accounts was not a popular choice. At one stage the canons, including Richard de Foston, with the help of John Verney, caused Cheswardine to flee for his life. It took the help of King Richard II to secure the abbot's position. Not that he was allowed a peaceful tenure. In 1385 John Cheswardine gave sanctuary to Ralph Becket and his companions who were indicted for the manslaughter of William Verney of Kingstone. No doubt Cheswardine was sympathetic to anyone who helped to even the score against the Verneys.

In the event Walter Osbern, Richard Foston, Richard Bakewell and John

Verney were arrested. It is likely that Cheswardine was also arrested because we learn of his pardon in 1387. It seems likely that they all gained their freedom, including Richard Bakewell, who succeeded Cheswardine as abbot in 1386.

Whether the disputes created so many diversions as to take the mind of the abbots away from the good management of the monastery or whether fines had been imposed as a result of the diversions, the abbey found itself, once again, in financial trouble. In 1399, the Sheriff of Staffordshire began an investigation into statements that the abbey was deeply in debt. Whatever the state of the abbey coffers the 140 years between then and the dissolution of the monastery in 1539 would seem ample time to make amends, but the abbey was reluctant to part with any of its income as may be seen from the records of *Valor Ecclisiasticus*.

The fact that they were taking moneys from the local church moved Hibbert to use the word 'robbed' in this connection. The following table indicates receipts of tithes to a value of £47-13-10 from which they paid a meagre 16 shillings and 8d to the local church.

	Tithes Received			Other Income from Churches			Payments to Churches		
	£	s.	d.	£	s.	d.	£	s.	d.
Brewood Nunnery									
Burton Abbey	46	6	8	52	13	4	4	6	8
						1			
Croxden Abbey	8	15	4				1	3	0
Dieulacres Abbey	57	19	8	10	10	8		18	6
Dudley Priory	18	16	8	2	6	0			
Hulton Abbey	18	10	0	2	0	0		5	4
Rocester Priory	47	13	10					16	8
St. Thomas's Priory	40	2	8	9	19	8		3	4
Stone Priory	53	10	0	22	8	0			
Trentham Priory	14	10	4	21	13	4			
Tutbury Priory	49	0	4	20	16	4	11	13	4
	£401	7	0	£141	19	5	£19	7	10

Receipts

	Glebe			Tithes			Easter Dues			Oblations		
	£	s	d	£	s	d	£	s	d	£	s	d
Rocester, Waterfall and Bradley				15	7	2						
Edensor (Derbysh.)				11	0	0						
Kynston				7	0	0						
Woodford (Northants)				13	6	8						

Not only was Rocester reluctant to part with its money it was not above the occasional error. One set of figures show a sum of £4.6s.8d. being paid to Lichfield Cathedral for the maintenance of a chantry there, although no trace of receipt is found in the Cathedral returns. On the other hand Rocester benefited from the bequest of John Fitzherbert of Norbury who left money in his will to the chantries at Rocester and Calwich.

The Archdeacons received annual visitation fees and fees for procurations. Once again we see that Rocester was not over generous.

	Bishop			Dean & Chapter			Archdeacon		
	£	s	d	£	s	d	£	s	d
Brewood Nunnery									
Burton Abbey	3	9	4½	6	13	4		17	9
Croxden Abbey							1	0	6
Dieulacres Abbey							1	2	0
Dudley Priory		(2)							
Hulton Abbey	2	1	10²′³		3	4		5	4
Rocester Priory							1	4	7
Ronton Priory	1	10	2²′³						
St. Thomas's Priory	3	6	9²′³	18	10	0	1	10	6
Stone Priory	1	8	6²′³	2	14	4		19	0
Trentham Priory	1	6	5²′³					13	4
Tutbury Priory		13	4	6	13	4	2	7	10
Total	£13	16	7⁵′⁶	£34	14	4	£10	0	10

When considering the income and expenditures it should be remembered that only a handful of canons were in permanent occupation. It was common practice to employ lay brethren to assist in the day to day running of the monastery and the husbandry of its demesne land. The lay brethren, often poorly educated, received minimal rewards, plus their keep, in return for their labour. In 1377 the monastic community, including the abbot, numbered six; in 1381 it was five; in 1524 it was seven, and at the time of the Dissolution the number was nine.

A visitation in 1524 showed the house to be efficiently run but with debts of £60 due to a payment to the Crown. It also noted that observation was generally satisfactory although the abbot complained that the brethren visited ale houses after divine services - poor or not, the brethren managed to pay for their pleasures.

As the Dissolution approaches we can take one last look at the abbey's income. The valuation of 1535 shows that the gross annual income of the house was £111.11s.7d. Whatever use the money was put to it did not prevent the abbot from trying to buy exemption from the Dissolution. A sum of £100 was paid to Lord Cromwell in an effort to have Rocester spared. It was to no avail. In 1538, Abbot Grafton and his eight canons were forced to surrender the monastery, with all its possessions, to the Crown. A pension of £13.6s.8d was assigned to the abbot.

The final year must have been harrowing for the abbot and canons. A letter survives in which the abbot makes his final plea to save the abbey.

The contents of the letter are reproduced on the next three pages:

The King to all to whom the present letters shall come, greeting.

Whereas by a certain Act in our Parliament begun at London on the third day of November in the twenty-first year of our reign, and then adjourned to Westminster, and by divers prorogations continued to the fourth day of February in the twenty-seventh year of our reign, and then held there, it was enacted amongst other things that we should have and enjoy for us and our heirs for ever all and singular monasteries priories and other religious houses of monks canons and nuns, by whatsoever kinds or diversities of rules or orders they should be had called or named, which had not lands tenements rents tithes portions and other hereditaments beyond the clear net yearly value of £200 , the said net yearly value of the said monasteries and priories to be taken and construed according to the net value certified in our Exchequer; and in like manner that we should have and enjoy for us and our heirs all and all manner of sites and circuits of the same religious houses, and all and singular manors granges messuages lands tenements reversions rents services tithes pensions portions advowsons patronages of churches (and) chapels annuitiee rights in-goings conditions and other hereditaments whatsoever pertaining or belonging to the same monasteries priories or religious houses not having, as is aforesaid, lands tenements or hereditaments beyond the aforesaid yearly value of £200 , as fully and entirely as the abbots priors abbesses and governors of such monasteries priories and other religious houses then had them or ought to have had them in right of their houses: To have and to hold all and singular the aforesaid, with all their rights profits jurisdictions and commodities, to us our heirs and successors for ever, therewith to do and use our proper will. Seeing, however, that in the said act it is provided that at any and whatsoever time after the making of that act we can and could at our pleasure ordain and appoint and declare by our letters patent to be made under our great seal that those and such of the said religious houses which we willed to be suppressed and dissolved should persevere and continue and remain in the same their corporate bodies and in the same their essential state quality condition force and effect, alike in their possessions and otherwise as they would be and would have been before the making of the act aforesaid, without the suppression or dissolution of the same, or of any part thereof, by pretext and authority of the same act, and that any such ordinance and declaration by us thus to be made and ordained should be good secure and effectual to the capital (i.e., chief) governors of such religious houses as we should not will to be suppressed and dissolved, and to their successors, after and according to the tenours and effects of the letters patent to be made therein, notwithstanding any thing or any things in the said act made to the contrary thereof, as in the said act is amongst other things more fully contained. Under pretext of which act the monastery or abbey of Blessed Mary of Rossetur in the diocese of Coventry and Lichfield, in our county of Stafford, for that it has not lands tenements rents tithes portions or hereditaments beyond the said net yearly value of £200 , as it may be certified in our said Exchequer and there doth plainly appear, is now in our hands and at our disposal as to whether it should be dissolved according to the form and effect of the act aforesaid, or should remain and continue in its pristine and essential state condition and quality, as it was before the making of the act aforesaid: Wishing therefore, the said monastery or abbey of Blessed Mary of Rossetur aforesaid, for divers causes and considerations at present specially moving us, to remain and continue in its pristine essential state body condition and quality, as it was before the making of the act aforesaid, and as it would be if that act had not been made, know therefore that we, on account of the favour which we bear and have towards the monastery of Blessed Mary of Rossetur aforesaid, which is not extended in its lands tenements and other hereditaments to the yearly value of £200, in the county aforesaid, of the order of Saint Augustine, in the diocese of Coventry and Lichfield, and in order that the abbot and the religious persons of the same monastery or abbey may attend more devoutly to celebrating divine worship therein, and may exercise more abundantly hospitality and other works of piety therein, have of our special grace and of our certain knowledge and mere motion, ordained appointed and declared, and by these presents, so far as in us lies, do ordain declare erect and renew, that the aforesaid monastery or abbey of Blessed Mary of Rossetur aforesaid shall for ever continue stand and remain in the same its corporate body, and in the same its essential state degree quality and condition, alike in its possessions and in all its other things, both in spirituals and in temporals, and mixed, as it was at the time of making of the act aforesaid, or at any time before the making of the said act, without any suppression or dissolution of the same monastery or abbey of Blessed Mary of Rossetur aforesaid, or of any part or parcel thereof, by force and authority of the act aforesaid. And further, of our special more abundant grace, we have granted and by these presents do grant that William Grafton, professed of the order of St. Augustine, shall be henceforth abbot of the said monastery or abbey of Blessed Mary of Rossetur aforesaid, and shall henceforth be held reputed and accepted as abbot and governor of the same monastery of Blessed Mary of Rossetur, in the same manner and form quality degree condition dignity state and strength, as the said William was on the fourth day of February in the twenty-seventh year of our reign, or before: and that all other religious persons of the same monastery or abbey of Blessed Mary of Rossetur aforesaid now being, or who were there on the fourth day of February in the said twenty-seventh year, and are now separated from the said convent, shall be in future and henceforth the convent of the same monastery or abbey of Blessed Mary of Rossetur aforesaid, and shall be held reputed and accepted henceforth for the convent of the same monastery or abbey of Rossetur aforesaid, in the same manner and form quality condition and state as they were on the said fourth day of February in the twenty-seventh year of our reign or before: and that the aforesaid William and the religious persons aforesaid, and all their successors, may and shall have the same succession in all things and by all things, as they had before the said fourth day of February in the said twenty-seventh year and ought to have had, and as they would have had and ought could or might have had if the act aforesaid had not been made: and that the aforesaid William, by the name of abbot of the said monastery or abbey of Blessed Mary of Rossetur, and his successors abbots of the monastery or abbey of Blessed Mary of Rossetur aforesaid, shall be henceforth persons able to plead and to be impleaded in all please suits plaints actions petitions, both real and personal and mixed, and any others soever in anysoever courts and places, and before anysoever judges or justices, alike spiritual and temporal, even though it touch us and our heirs, and to do exercise and execute all and singular other things whatsoever, as abbot of the said monastery or abbey of Blessed Mary of Rossetur aforesaid, as they might have done and could have done before the making of that act, and as they might have done and could have done if that act had been in no wise made and put forth: and that the aforesaid William and the religious persons aforesaid, as the abbot and convent of the monastery or abbey of Blessed Mary (of) Rossetur aforesaid, and their successors, abbots and convent(s) of that monastery or abbey, shall have enjoy and hold, and may and can have for ever, all the aforesaid monastery or abbey of Blessed Mary of Rossetur aforesaid, and also the church bell-tower site cemetery soil and precincts of the same church, and all and singular our manors messuages lands tenements rents reversions services possessions pensions perpetuities and hereditaments whatsoever, and also commodities ornaments jewels goods and chattels and other things whatsoever, both spiritual and temporal, belonging or pertaining to the same monastery or abbey, in the same manner and form as they would have enjoy and hold them or might and could have had enjoyed and held them, if the act aforesaid had not been made and put forth. And for giving greater security of and in the aforesaid to the aforesaid abbot and convent of the monastery or abbey of Blessed Mary *of Rossetur aforesaid, and to their successors, know further that we, of our special more abundant grace, have given and granted, and by these presents do give and grant, to the aforesaid abbot of the same monastery or abbey of Blessed Mary of Rosseur aforesaid, and to the convent of the same place, and to their successors, all the said monastery or abbey of Blessed Mary of Rossetur aforesaid, and also all the site soil precincts church bell-tower and cemetery of the same monastery or abbey aforesaid, and all and singular demesnes manors messuages lands tenements woods underwoods rents reversions services knights fees wardships marriages reliefs escheats parks warrens pools ponds fishponds commons rectories vicarages advowsons and patronages of churches chapels and chantries lands glebes pensions portions tithes oblations courts-leet views of frank-pledge liberties jurisdictions franchises and other rights possessions and hereditaments whatsoever, and all goods and chattels bells jewels ornaments and other things whatsoever to the same monastery or abbey of Blessed Mary of Rossetur aforesaid belonging or pertaining, and which the aforesaid abbot and convent on the fourth day of February in the said twenty-seventh year, or before or after, in right of that monastery or abbey had held or enjoyed, and which by reason and pretext of the act aforesaid have and ought to have come to our hands, as fully and entirely, and in as ample manner and form, as the said abbot and convent on the said fourth day of February in the said twenty-seventh year before the making of the aforesaid act, in right of the monastery or abbey aforesaid, had held or enjoyed them and as fully and entirely, and in as ample manner and form as they by reason pretext vigour or authority of the act aforesaid came and ought to have come to our hands, and in our hands now are or ought to be: to have hold and enjoy the aforesaid monastery or abbey of Blessed Mary of Rossetur aforesaid, and all and singular the other things aforesaid, with all their rights appurtenances and commodities, to the aforesaid William, abbot of the said monastery or abbey, and to the convent of the same place, and to their successors, in pure and perpetual alms for ever, of us our heirs and successors, as of our foundation, and not otherwise: paying to the chief lords of the lands and tenements aforesaid and of the other things aforesaid, and of each parcel thereof, the rents and services due therefor, and by law accustomed, to them and to each of them: provided always that the aforesaid abbot and convent by unanimous consent, for them and their successors, grant by these presents to us and our heirs that the aforesaid abbot and convent and their successors forever shall pay and cause to be paid to us, our heirs and successors, all tithes and first fruits, as often as they shall happen to arise, in the same manner and form as if the aforesaid monastery or abbey had not been suppressed dissolved or given to us by the act aforesaid, and according to the force form and effect of a certain act of Parliament put forth and provided for tithes and first fruits. And the said abbot and convent grant by these presents that they and their successors for ever shall well and faithfully keep and observe all and all manner of rules ordinances constitutions and statutes to be provided assigned and appointed concerning or touching the good government of the same monastery or abbey and the religious persons of the same monastery or abbey, by us, as Supreme Head of the Church of England, or by our ministers and successors. And furthermore we will grant these our letters patent, to be made in the form aforesaid, under our great seal, without in any wise paying or doing fine or fee, great or small, in the hanaper of our Chancery for the aforesaid or any of the aforesaid for our use. And that express mention etc. In witness of which etc. Witness the King at Westminster on the eleventh day of March in the twenty-ninth year of the reign of King Henry the Eighth. By the King himself etc.*

Endorsed   (In a contemporary hand):   Continuacion of Abbey de Rouster.
11th. March 29th Hen. 8th.

The fact that the abbot's letter failed to win a reprieve should come as no surprise. Henry VIII's break with Rome may well have been the result of religious dogma but personal gain was also high on the agenda. Rich or poor, the overall value of the monasteries with their lands and possessions, offered excellent pickings. It was not only Henry who sought to gain but also those appointed to carry out the task. To deal with treasure that would accrue to the Crown, a Court of Augmentation was created. To oversee the Dissolution a chancellor was appointed. He was supported by a treasurer, an attorney and solicitor, ten auditors and seventeen receivers and various clerks.

It was the job of the chancellor, Sir Richard Riche, the Solicitor General, to control the surrenders and to dispose of all property and moveables. The treasurer was Sir Thomas Pope and amongst the auditors was William Cavendish. The receiver for the Staffordshire area was John Scudamore. The passing of the Act of Dissolution was the signal for a scramble for spoils, a golden opportunity for personal gain. It was grasped by those entrusted to value, audit and dispose of monastic wealth, but if crimes were committed or favour extracted they seem to have been overlooked or made light of. Cavendish benefited enormously from the Dissolution by 'acquiring' lands in Doveridge.

On 23rd August, Cranmer wrote to Cromwell urging the suppression of Tutbury, Rocester and Croxden. This, despite the fact that all three had paid for their continuance only a year earlier. Cranmer, it appears, was eager for Croxden to pass to his servant Francis Bassett. Cavendish and Legh, a fellow auditor, went about their business in earnest. They arrived at Tutbury in September 1538 where the deed of surrender was signed on the 14th of that month. The relationship between Tutbury and Doveridge is well defined and Cavendish would have found it easy enough to annex the Doveridge estates when Tutbury was handed over to the Crown.

From Tutbury, Cavendish and Legh proceeded to Rocester and Croxden. Rocester signed the deed of surrender on the 16th of September and Croxden signed on the 17th. The signatories for Rocester consist of the Abbot and his eight canons.

> Wylliamum Grafton
> Georgium Dave
> Johannum Snape
> Ricardum Heith
> Johannum Brykylbake
> Radulphum Corke
> Wylliamum Bond
> Georgium Grafton
> Johannum Dayne

The following witnesses also signed;

> Mr (Magister) Williamus Bassett, miles
> Thomas Fizharberd, armiger
> William Bassett, armiger
> Johannes Fizharberd, generosies

Briefly the deed reads as follows:

And memorandum that on the day and year aforesaid the said abbot and convent came before Thomas Legh, Doctor of Law, in the chapter house of the same abbot and convent and acknowledged the deed aforesaid and all and singular contained therein in the form aforesaid!

Given the 16th day of month of September in the year of our Lord 1538.

Hard on the heels of Cavendish and Legh followed Scudamore who promptly arranged a public auction. The sale at Rocester took place on the 16th October. It was a short affair as very little was sold except for St. Michael's Chapel. John Forman purchased *'the glasse and iron in the wyndowes'* for three shillings and sixpence. William Loghortonhouse purchased the timber from the chapel for seven shillings and sixpence and William Bagnall bought the *'shyngle'* for eightpence. The total purchase was just eleven shillings and sixpence.

The parishioners obtained three bells because they had been rung for village services as well as for those of the canons. No mention is made of the silver gilt communion cup or the pewter used in the house. The house and site of the monastery were leased in March 1539 to Edward Draycot, one of Cromwell's servants, for twenty one years, but was sold the following year to Richard Trentham. The sale included a chamber and church yard belonging to the vicarage of Rocester.

After the dissolution of the lesser abbeys the commission moved on to those whose values exceeded £200. Burton was dissolved and made into a collegiate church with Abbot Edie as Dean. Abbots and monks from Staffordshire houses struggled for survival. The fate of all is not known but some became parish priests or retired on small pensions. Others became schoolmasters or clerks, or entered into professions worthy of their status.

As for William Cavendish, he completed his task and continued to make good his family fortunes. Cavendish appeared briefly to have to answer for his penchant for extracting financial reward from various monasteries. It seems that spending was somewhat lavish at Brewood and that the path of the auditors was strewn with gifts. Cavendish accepted higher rewards and wages than he had divulged. The acceptance of bribes was common practice and both Cavendish and Legh confessed to the king that it was true. In 1541 the sum of £3. 10s. 00d was paid to sundry witnesses who came to the Court of Augmentation to give evidence for the king against Cavendish and Legh.

Whatever the result, a fine or reprimand, it made little difference. The king benefited greatly from the spoils of dissolution, as did the chancellor, treasurer, auditors and receivers. Complaints against his commissioners were unlikely to make any difference. Cavendish completed his task - and amassed his wealth.

Sources

Victoria History of Staffordshire Vol. II
Dissolution of the Monasteries. Hibbert 1969
History of Denstone. Tom Goode

FOUR
ST. MICHAEL'S CHURCH & ITS INCUMBENTS

The history of the village church is difficult to ascertain if only because of frequent changes that have occurred throughout the life of the village itself. A reference to a church is noted in the foundation charter of the abbey in 1141. *'Richard gave to Thurston, the first Abbott, and to his canons, the church of Rocester'*. A further reference occurred in 1229 when Bishop Stavensby gave the abbey permission to appropriate the church of Rocester. The church referred to would have been St. Michael's as the abbey had its own church. Further 13th century conclusions can be drawn from the shaft of a damaged cross that stands in the churchyard. However, with a little conjecture, a case can be made for the church to have been established long before the formal references.

If we consider the religious activities of the 6th century and the growing influence of Christianity it appears inconceivable that Rocester would have been neglected. Even in the aftermath of its Roman heyday it would have remained a sizeable trading community and as such would have attracted the attention of religious pioneers. Commonsense alone suggests that Rocester would have had a church and a priest.

What then do we make of the Domesday Book? Although a church is not always mentioned in the entries it is a surprising omission from such a large village. It may well be that Rocester was razed to the ground in the post conquest rebellions in the area. Rebellions were common and both Rocester and Uttoxeter resisted, albeit briefly, the Norman overlords. If that were the case, the church may have still been in ruins and only rebuilt after the survey of 1086.

Significantly we can relate the church of St. Michael with the abbey of St. Mary for we know that they stood side by side. St. Michael's, whilst independent, worked in tandem with the conventual church of the abbey to serve the people of Rocester. The activities of the abbey overshadowed the stability of the village church but despite the turmoil of abbey life and the antics of the canons, St. Michael's not only survived but outlived the abbey. For four hundred years abbey and church stood side by side, until Henry VIII brought about the split with Rome and set in motion the Dissolution of the Monasteries.

That the church of St. Michael and the abbey of St. Mary were separate entities is without question. Even so the church did not escape unscathed. Whilst the abbey faced terminal decline physically, and rapid decline spiritually, the church suffered only physical damage. Both conventual church and abbey met the same fate when they were sold to the highest bidder. Fortuitously, whether legally or illegally, the valuables of the village church were not included in the sale. The glass windows, the timbers and the shingles that formed part of the auction were ultimately replaceable. The church treasures would have been far more difficult to replace.

An inventory taken on 8th May 1553 reveals the full extent of the valuables that in 1538 were removed for their safe keeping.

1 silver chalice with patern, 4 Vestments, 2 Albes, 1 Bruges satin cape, 1 pair of brass censers, 1 ship, 1 brass bucket, 1 brass pyx, 1 pewter cruet, 2 corporals, 3 altercloths for short alters, 3 bells, 1 sacring bell, 1 handbell, 2 crosses.
Church Wardens James Les and Thomas Greene.

The inclusion of a silver chalice is of interest for it may well be the silver gilt communion cup that the king gave to the abbey of St. Mary in 1246.

From the list of incumbents it is apparent that St. Michael's was quickly restored to its former glory and fulfilling its accustomed role. No vacancies are recorded immediately after 1538 and it appears that the vicars Thomas Mecocke and his successor John Garbett ensured the smooth transition to the religious life of post-dissolution.

For over three centuries the old church witnessed the course of history, and taking in its stride a number of structural changes, it managed to survive until 1870 before being almost totally replaced.

Our picture of the pre-1870 church is taken from a drawing produced by a Rocester parishioner. From this picture, and from the church records we can deduce a little of the history of St. Michael's between 1538 and 1870.

By general consensus the tower is of 13th century origin, although modified. A filled-in arched window is still very evident but the castellans on the top of the tower are not apparent. Four pinnacles and a weather vane gave the tower a pleasant symmetry.

The perimeter plans and internal layout of the old church add to the mystery rather than resolve it. The tower is noticeably off centre. The broad dimensions of the main body of the church appear to be about 55 feet by 50 feet if the apse is not included. Consequently the absence of internal supports lead to speculation as to whether the roof could span 50 feet.

The black spots indicate the cast iron pillars used to support a loft or gallery that was erected in 1784. It could be that the original church building of the 12th century was much smaller and more symmetrical with the tower. No faculty records exist to support such suppositions. Neither do records exist to show the expansions that almost certainly did take place.

By examining the roof, the windows and the raised door, logic points to specific conclusions. The position of the rain spouts indicate that the roof did not span the entire width of the church. Instead it stopped some distance short of the outer wall. From the outer wall it seems likely that a short, low angled roof would form a valley with the inverted V shape of the central roof. Rain water would run along the valley and enter the down spouts on each side of the apse. Despite the fact that supports are not seen on the plans they would certainly have been required.

The small door, with the access steps, was built into the north wall in 1784 and led to a gallery, as indicated in two faculties granted around that time.

Faculty - Ref. B/C/5/1761/7 4th January 1761

A citation was read during divine service at Rocester by Thomas Sherwin, minister. The document was from Richard Smalbroke, doctor of Laws, Vicar General - Lichfield and Coventry on behalf of Stephen Watson and Thomas Orme, Churchwardens. The churchwardens being desirous to build a loft or gallery for six seats or pews in a vacant place at the west end of the church, quite across the isles (sic) thereof to contain twenty two feet in breadth from north to south and to extend from wall of the west end of the floor of the church twelve feet in length towards the east. From the bottom of the front to the loft to be eight feet in height. For several parishioners not already accommodated with seats or pews. Also for singers. With stairs leading into loft gallery on north side. Seats marked 1,2,3,4 and 5. Seat 1 for Thomas Biddulph, 2 for William Horsley, 3 for John Barnet and John Lownds jointly, 4 for William Micock, 5 for Thomas Orm and the several respective families so long as they live in Rocester. Number 6 for the use of singers.

Dated 30th December 1760

Whether the faculty was acted upon or not, is difficult to ascertain, but a further faculty was granted in 1784. The citation, dated 8th May 1784, was signed by the vicar Joseph Clowes. This time Richard Smalbroke granted to Thomas Bainbridge and Thomas Wilkinson the right *"to erect a commodious gallery with seats and fittings on the north side, eight feet eight inches from the north wall to the isle (sic), to be supported by light and finial iron pillars with two spacious seats therein, one for Thomas Bainbridge and his family and one for Thomas Wilkinson and his family. Also to make a staircase and door in north wall with steps from the churchyard."* The churchwardens are named as John Armshaw and John Watson.

The windows in the drawing are very similar in design to those in other local churches where a more precise date is known. Pevsner's illustration of Longnor church (1780) shows almost identical windows. Forton church, of a similar date, displays similar windows which were much in vogue at the time. The conclusion from this would be that the windows in St. Michael's were added between 1780 and 1874. More realistically, a date of 1823 would tie in with an unsubstantiated reference found in a brief history of St. Michael's Church and Parish which refers to a church enlargement in that year. Assuming the enlargement of the church in 1823 to be correct it is surprising that a decision was taken to rebuild the church completely in 1871. The citation dated 3rd May 1871 was formed at the request of the vicar Rev. Wray

Richard Hunt Clerk M.A. and the churchwardens Minton Campbell and Arthur Finch Dawson. John Sutcliffe is recorded as assistant overseer:

Take down and remove the whole of the present church of Rocester (with the exception of the tower walls) together with all the pews, seats and sitting places and rebuild the said church and chancel as shown on the said plan. To erect a new porch and vestry and to erect a spire on the present tower. Remove also vestry, reading desk, galleries and chancel monuments. Vault Tablets etc. to remain in a suitable place.

The cost was to be met by voluntary subscription and the document was signed by William Fell, Registrar.

The architect chosen for the rebuilding was Ewan Christian. A popular choice at the time, Christian's work was much in evidence locally and therefore readily available for the vicar and churchwardens to examine at first hand before selecting him to design the new church. The cost of rebuilding was about £4,000 and was met in part by Mr. C. M. Campbell, who contributed £400 and also the east window. Large donations were also received from Sir Percival Haywood, Bart. and the Houlsworth family. Mr Campbell also gave the organ. Mrs Dawson contributed a beautiful inlaid altar and Mrs Webb of Clownholme gave a number of books.

The postcard picture shows the church prior to the collapse of the weir that fed the cotton mills. It is thought that when the weir collapsed in 1943 the local water table was lowered quite dramatically. As a result, ground movement caused considerable subsidence in parts of the village. The end section of the church developed serious cracking in the side walls and would need substantial renovation. Instead it was decided to reduce the length of the church, rebuild the end gable, and reinstall the windows.

St Michael's. Redesigned and rebuilt in 1871.

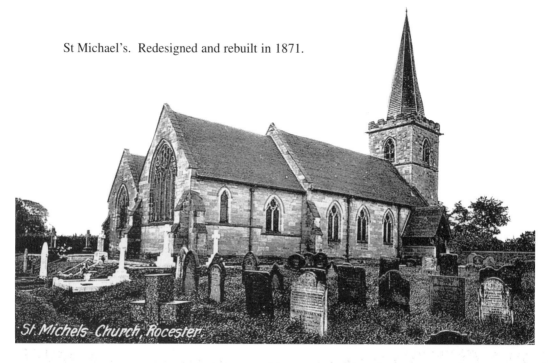

St. Michels Church, Rocester.

The result of all this is a pleasant if unspectacular church that fits well enough into the unpretentious Staffordshire village that Rocester is. It was described as follows by D. J. Sinken in 1983 :

The Lych Gate

Victorian furnishings inside. The 13th century tower has blocked up circular headed windows, is castellated with three plain string courses and a moulded string course with four gargoyles. The nave, with its centre aisle, is separated from the south aisle by a three pointed arcade with short polished marble columns with naturalistic capitols. There are three, three light windows in the south wall, and three, two light windows in the north wall. All with stained glass. The west window of the south aisle is three lights, the centre having fragments of old glass. The font and circular stone pulpit are both Victorian. The east window has five lights and is attributed to de-Morgan. There are two stained glass windows in the north wall of the chancel consisting of two lights and one light respectively.

Several monuments are mentioned as well as the 13th century cross and steps in the church yard. Simkin makes no mention of the church bells nor to the repairs and restoration of the west windows.

In June 1972 a centenary appeal was launched by the Rev. J. D. Cutter BD and the churchwardens, L. J. Parsons and T. Grant, to raise £400 for restoration. The architects were Wood, Goldstone and Yorath of Hanley, and the glasswork was by Weir Glass of Hanley. The faculty was readily granted and for the sum of £398 Weir agreed to, *remove all existing panels including tracery, to supply and lead in a new memorial panel to approved design, to strengthen existing stained glass panel and reposition. Antique diamond panels to be changed for rectangular ......To include words, totally renewed. "A Thank Offering For Church Restoration 1972".*

The bells of Rocester, St. Michael's, are listed as follows:

N. Blews & Sons founders Birmingham 1871.
Peace and good neighbourhood 1774
Fear God honour the King 1774
Prosperity to the Parish 1774
Thos Gould Church Warden
Edwd Arnold Leicester fecit 1796
I Rudhall fect 1830

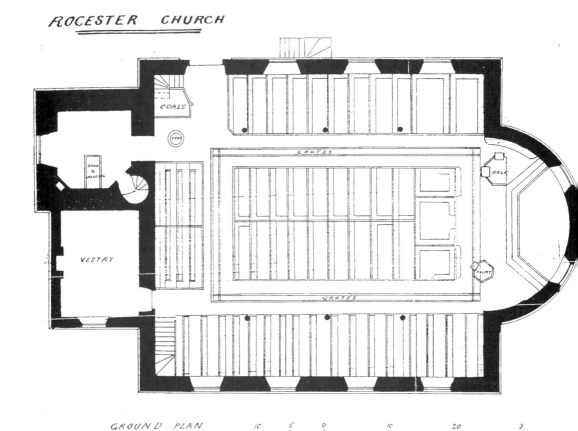

ROCESTER CHURCH

GROUND PLAN

55'

GALLERY PLAN

The plan of the old church.

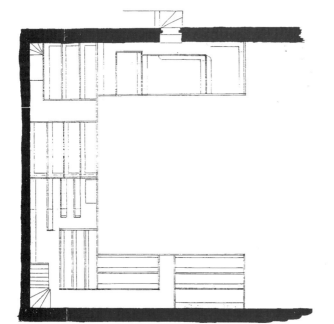

Left: The gallery in the old church.

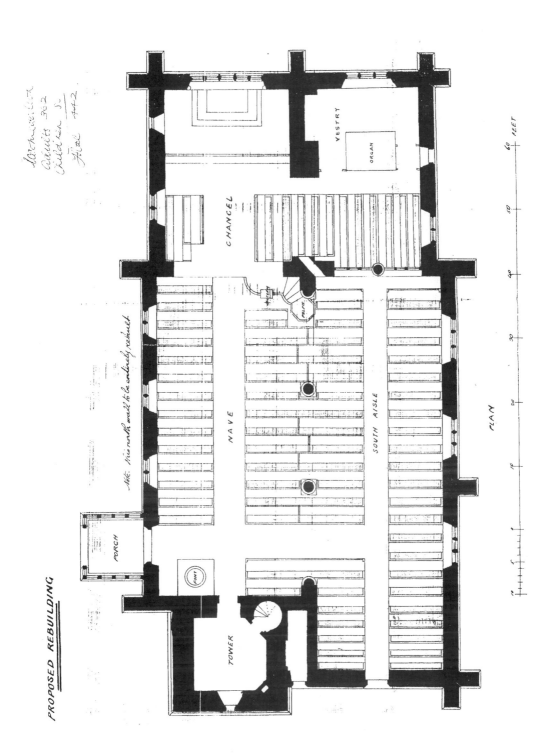

The plans for the proposed new church, 1871.

Incumbents of St. Michael's church

For the most part the canons of St. Mary also took on the role of vicar to the parish. In some instances the canon who presided as the vicar would succeed the abbot.

The following list is compiled from three sources; the entry in Staffordshire Parish Registers differs slightly from the Staffordshire Historical Collection; both show a variation from the Victorian County History. The list uses dates as a precedent.

V	1142	Thurstan	
V	1146	Ivo	
V	1155	Richard	
V	1210	Henry	
V	1215	William	Occurs between 1215 and 1224
	1227	Henry	
V	1238	Philip	
V	1256	Richard	
V	1258	Walter	Resigned 1269
V	1269	Walter de Dodele	
	1274	Nicholas	
	1275	John	
V	1286	Robert	Died 1289
	1288	John	
V	1289	Roger of Loughborough	} probably the same
	1300	Roger	
	1302	Robert	
	1305	Roger de Lughteburgh	Roger again.
V	1316	Walter of Aston	Vicar in 1312
V	1324	Gilbert de Bosco	Vicar in 1317
V	1335	Henry of Hopton	
V	1349	William of Cheadle	
V	1364	Thomas of Rocester	
V	1367	John Cheswardine	
V	1386	Robert of Bakewell	
V	1407	Henry Smyth	
V	1443	John Hambury	
V	1466	Robert Twys	
V	1475	John Quinten (Quynton)	
V	1486	George Caldon	
		William Butler	
V		William John	Died 1507
V	1507	Roger Rolleston alias Stathum	
V		Thomas Bromley	Occurs 1521
V		William Grafton	Occurs 1524
			Surrendered the abbey in 1538
	1533	Thomas Mecocke, Vicar, probably the anticipated successor to Grafton.	
	1549	John Garbet	

1558/9	Richard Sewer
1559	William Okeden
1560/63	A Vicar - unnamed
1563	Peter Mynsh
1565	Robert Smith
1621	Thomas Holmes BA
1640	Thomas Bently
1645	John Hill
1677	Elias Poynton
1699	Geo Lindley
1699	Brian Harding
1743	Thomas Sherwin
1776	Joseph Clowes
1786	William Eddowes
1791	Joseph Clowes
1798	Thomas Bainbridge
1802	John Langley
1820	George Hake
1849	William Holloway
1851	John Chippendale
1855	Lorenzo Moore
1857	Warden F. Stubbs
1869	Wray Richard Hunt
1892	Maurice George Lascalle
1897	W. C. Wright

12th century cross shaft in
Rocester churchyard

Following the date of the surrender of the Abbey, the lists from the Staffordshire Historical Society and the Parish Records coincide except for the name Geo Lundley 1699 which is not included in the Parish Records. The date 1699 coincides with the arrival of Brian Harding who remained until 1743. Lundley may have been a temporary incumbent and not considered as a replacement for Elias Poynton (1677 to 1699)

When considering the list of incumbents it must be recognised that the compilers of the Victorian County Histories refer to original sources wherever possible. Some references, where the origin is in doubt, lead to a degree of uncertainty. The Parish Records compare proofs with the Lichfield transcripts but nevertheless require laborious study of original entries that are made in a variety of written styles and legibility. The Victorian County Histories follow a more defined and logical route.

Sources
V = Victorian County History line of succession.
County Archives - Stafford
William Salt Library - Stafford

The church today, the Abbey Farm and the Old Vicarage.

FIVE
VILLAGE RECORDS

In many ways the people of Rocester suffered more from poverty than did the cannons of St. Marys. In the aftermath of the Dissolution, Rocester displays all the signs of desperation so common with the times. Parish registers kept by the church wardens and the records of the overseer of the poor make grim reading.

A ledger, entitled *Old Parish Registers of Rocester*, records entries from 1564 and offers an interesting glimpse of life in the village. H. Flacket, Church Warden, notes the first entry thus:

Richard Smith 1564, the first day (XIX) January of my serving the cure of Rocester.

The second entry records an unusual event, a double marriage on both male and female sides:

1567. Marriages of Richard Colclough, Gent to Dorothy Madeley and Bartholomew Colclough to Elizabeth Madeley.

Further selected entries are:

1597. Buried T. Madeley, Gent.

1598. A poor woman was buried whose name we know not. She was brought into the town from Ellastone. Robert Smyth cure.

1607. Lady dies on a visit.

1609. W. H. drowned.

1612. Roger, a beggar's son, baptised.

1614. W. Chetwynd married Ellen Freares.

1638. Buried W. Chetwynd.

1674. Collected for Nathan in Rocester church. 10s - 2d

1688. Marriage of strangers by licence.

1699. Quarterly session of the Peace held at Stafford on Tuesday the week following after St. Michael the Archangel. Upon the (instructions)? of Willm Cotton esq. a gratuity of £30 was granted for the building of Churnet Bridge in Rocester.

1709. Poor traveller died in cottage barn at Clownholme.

1714. A poor child died in towne street.

1776. A black-a-moor buried.

The accounts of the Overseer are involved with the upkeep of the poor:

Accounts of John Arnold, Overseer of the poor in the hamlet of Rocester from Easter 1790 to Easter 1791:

Paid George Evans for wood and work for William Harrisons house	*£6 - 7s - 0d*
Paid for 2,500 bricks	*£2 - 0s - 0d*
Paid George Hill the older when his wife was ill	*£0 - 7s - 0d*

Paid George Hill the younger for cotton that was burnt	£1 - 6s - 0d
Paid Margaret Braddock for curing George Hills child	£0 - 5s - 0d

James Richardson, Overseer 1791-1792:

Paid for coffing for Hannah Shenton	£0 - 12s - 0d
Paid for two pair of shoes for Shentons	£0 - 6s - 0d

The Shentons and the Hills were regular recipients of aid and were among the poorest of Rocester's inhabitants. The overseer, ever mindful of the cost of illness and death, recorded their own medical remedies. Some of the remedies, based on herbal applications, may well have proved beneficial. Others appear to be based more on folklore than reality:

An essence for the head ache.
Head aches are sometimes caused from an obnoxious vapour ascending from the stomach which in this case must be cleansed by proper remedies, but for the common headache take of French Brandy, or rectified spirits of wine, one quart, put it into a strong bottle and add one ounce of camphor cut small, a quarter of an ounce of essence of lemon and two ounces of the strongest volatile spirit of sal-ammoniac. Stop the bottle quite close and shake it three or four times a day for a week. The method of using it is to rub the hand with a little of it and hold it hard upon the part afflicted until it is dry. If the pain is not quite removed, repeat until it is.

A cure for piles or sores.
Eat Rosemary and Sage with bread and butter and apply wheat flour and honey by way of a plaster

How to cure warts.
Go into the field and take a black snail, and rub them with the same nine times one way and then nine times another, and then stick the said snail upon a block and the warts will waste.

Another major problem for the overseer, and one that could not be cured by medicinal means, was the incidence of pregnancy amongst the females of the village. The fact that an unmarried mother would produce a bastard child meant a financial strain on the parish purse. The overseers did their utmost to discourage such acts. Not that they had much success. Nature, plus lack of contraception and a lack of education, resulted in the inevitable consequences.

The records show little tact or sympathy. Every unmarried pregnancy was closely examined and commented upon. The records of so called voluntary examination are short and to the point:

County of Stafford. Under oath, Elizabeth Robinson of Sudbury in Derbyshire and now in Rocester is with child and the said child is likely to be born a bastard, and that Joseph Evans of Sudbury is the father of the said child.

Henrietta Harrison of Rocester - a widow woman, swore on oath before Clement Kynnersly Esq. Justice of the Peace on 10th. March 1783 that she was delivered of a female bastard child on 19th. December 1782 and the child is likely to become chargeable to the said parish. John Saunders of Rocester, a maltster did get her with child.

More stark and elaborate was the case of Robotta Payser:

The examination of Robotta Payser - single woman of Quickshell gave birth to Margaret and that William Shipton of Tutbury was the father and that sometime in the Hay Harvest last had carnal knowledge of her body at Tutbury and did beget her with child.

The father of the child was subjected to similar pressures as the overseers tried everything within their power to place responsibility where it lay. If the constable was required to apprehend the father then so be it.

Moving to another parish to make a fresh start was not an easy option either. If you were incumbent upon one parish you became incumbent upon the other. The overseer was most reluctant to accept problems from another parish. So much so that legal transfers had to be applied for and approved by both sides before being granted by a local magistrate. If you were financially independent you had the privilege of freedom. If you were poor and dependent upon charity it was virtually impossible to escape this poverty trap.

When the numbers of poor people reached a level beyond the financial capability of the parish, paupers were transferred to the workhouse. Despite the stigma attached to the workhouse the inmates were often better off than those living in the parish slums. Rocester used the workhouse at Ipstones on a regular basis from 1766 onwards and by 1816 were also sending their poor to Caverswall.

A public meeting in Rocester in 1816 agreed to send the poor of Rocester to Caverswall workhouse and to pay Joseph Collier, yeoman, the sum of £15 as salary and rent for the workhouse, and a further sum of 2s-6d weekly for each person sent by the Rocester Church Warden and Overseer. The use of Caverswall workhouse was formalised by a legal agreement organised by Thomas Palmby, Churchwarden, Joseph Salt, Overseer for the Township and F. Salt. The Justices of the Peace were Lord Waterpark of Doveridge and Mark Anthony, who formalised the document in the court at Stafford.

The use of the workhouse may well have eased the workload on the overseer, but the treatment of unmarried mothers and their bastard children was more a matter of attitude. The poor and destitute were equally dependent on the parish. The Hills and the Shentons produced legitimate children but they were just as dependent on the parish. The workhouse was a distinct possibility for any of them.

What is clear from an examination of parish records throughout history is the gulf between the haves and the have-nots. The following is dated 31st May 1602 :

"made in the Court of the Lady the Queen, at Westminster, on the morrow of the holy trinity in the year of the reign of Elizabeth, by grace of God Queen of England, France and Ireland, Defender of the faith, between William Fawne, querent and Richard Buckley alias Bucklowe and Helen his wife":

One messuage, two cottages, two gardens, two orchards, twenty acres of land, ten acres of meadow, seventy acres of pasture, four acres of woodland and common pasture with appurtenances in Clownam, Sedsal, Eaton and Doveridge, and of free fishing on the waters of the Dove.

All for the sum of 130 marks of silver.

Records of baptism are also interesting. The oldest entry is:

Thomas. f.s. of Ricardi and Agnetis Nashe. 1st. of March 1566.

And in 1566 we note the baptisms:

Andre. f.s. Ricardi et Helen Meave
Helene. f.d. Thomas Wolriche
Edwardus. f.s. Randulphi and Agnetis Buckley de Clownam.

Buckley and Clownam are still well known in the Rocester area. Other names have links with the past. Volume 1 of the Parish Registers records the baptism of *Vere. d. of Francis and Catherine Trentham in 1599.* The Trenthams acquired the estates previously belonging to the abbey of St. Mary.

Also mentioned in the baptism records is *Bacon. 1586, January 4th. Joanes d. of John and Helene Bacon jnr.* The Bacons were almost certainly descendants of Richard Bacon who founded the abbey in the 12th century.

The Botts and the Harrisons appear frequently through the centuries and are equally prominent today indicating the remarkable stability among local families:

Volume II

   1705 June 10   Marriage of Thomas Bott and Ann Berrisford.

Volume III

   1812 December 24th.   Marriage of Thomas Tarn and Ellen Harrison.

Village records also list typical rents and, surprisingly, a nice tradition when the landlord gave his tenants a capon each Christmas. *Rocester rents Lady Day 1700:*

	£	s	d
M. Woodnot	00	5	00
Thomas Godhelp	00	13	04
Elizabeth Sladen	00	11	06
Thomas Nash	00	10	06
Edward Stone	00	7	00
William Godrich	00	14	04
Margaret Kemp	00	10	00
Francis Adams	00	13	04
Gent	00	7	00
William Taylor	00	16	00
Alice Pakeman	00	6	08
George & Robert Braddock	00	6	08
George Ball	00	5	00
Braddock	00	0	06
Richard Botham	00	5	00
	7	16	02

Two views of Woodseat Hall

Pedigree of Trentham of Rocester.

Harl; *MSS*, 1570.[24], 6128.[11].
Erdeswicke; *Bakewell, and Leek Registers; Old Deed, dated* 7 *July*, 1619.

ARMS.—*Arg.*, 3 griffins' heads erased
sa, beaked *gu*.

William Trentham, of = —— d. Horton, de
Shrewsbury, Armiger. | Woodcote, co. Salop.

John Trentham, of Shrews- = Sister and h. Willi Hoord,
bury, esq., supstes, 23° Ed. | of Shrewsbury.
IV., aᵒ. Di. 1483.

Thomas Trentham, sen., of = Katharine, f' and h. John
Shrewsbury, esq., 17° Hen. | Mareshall, of Hurst, co.
VII. | Salop.

Thomas Trentham, jun., of = Elizabeth, f' Richard Corbett, of
Shrewsbury, esq., aᵒ. 1502. | Moreton, Salop, militis.

Ricardus Trentham, of Shrewsbury, esq., = Mary, d. David
cup-bearer (pocillitor) to Edward VI.; had | Ireland, of co.
grant of Rocester priory, aᵒ. 1540, 31₀ Hen. | Salop.
VIII.

Joanna, ux. Godfrey	Thomas Trentham, M.P., = Jana, d. Sir William	Joyce, ux. Edmund	Margaret, ux. Sampson
Foljambe, of Norton-	for Newcastle-under-Lyme, Sneyd, of Bradwell, and	Mynors, of Utcester.	Meverell, of Throwley.
Lees, Derb.	1580-1; of Rocester; supstes of Keele, Knt. ob.	=	=
=	aᵒ. Di. 1583.		∧

Elizabeth, ux. 2. = Edward Vere, 17th Earl	Francis Trentham, of Rocester, 1583-'99, = Katharine, d. Ralph Sheldon,	Katharine = Sir John Stan-
maid of honour	of Oxford; wit, patriot,	sheriff of Staffordshire, 1593, living, 1619.	of Beeley, co. Worcester.	Trentham,	hope, of Shel-
"pedisequa," to	&c. Commander in ex-			ux. 2.	ton and Elvas-
Queen Elizabeth.	pedition against Arma-				ton, ob. 1610.
	da, 1588; introduced	Sir Thomas Trentham, = Prudentia, d.	Sir Xtopher	William.		
	perfumes at Court; ob.	of Rocester, Knt. e. s.	Thos. Eyre,	Trentham, of	Anthony, living,		1608.
	aᵒ. 1604.	and h. living, 1619.	of Hasop,	yᵉ Dayry-	1619.	Mary, d. Sir = Sir John Stan- = Olivia, d.
			esq., nd.	house, Horton,	Rafe Trentham,	John Ratcliffe	hope, of Elvas-	h. Edward
Henry de Vere, 18th Earl of Oxford,		Bakevell,	near Leek,	bp. Leek, 1605.	of Ordsall,	ton, Kntd., aᵒ.	Beresford
lord great-chamberlain; o.s.p. at		1619, ob.	1644, o.s.p.		ux. 2.	1607, ob. 1638.	Beresford,
siege of Breda, aᵒ. 1605, æt.		Westwood,					1591.
		Leek, 1642,			John Stanhope,	Olive Stanhope, = Charles
		sep. Rocester.			s. and h. æt. 9	s. d. and h. to	of Ovi
	Sir Francis Trentham, of = Elizabeth, e. d. Sir Wm. Bowyer,		October, 1627,	her mother; ob.	co. Sus
	Rocester, only s. and h.	of Knypersley and Silway; (remd.		à quo, Earls of	aᵒ. æt. 38.	1658.
		John Bowyer, vicar of Biddulph.)		Harrington.		
				=	
	Elizabeth Trentham, (ob. 1713,) only = Bryan Cockayne 2d Viscount Cullen,		∧	
	d. and h. (à quâ, yᵉ Viscounts Cullen,	of Ireland; of Rocester, 1660 (had			1656.
	extinct on death of Borlase Cullen,	with his wife Rocester and Castle-Hed-		Charles Cotton, yᵉ poet- = Isabella, d. Sir Thos. Hutc
	6th Viscount, who ob. cælebs, 1813.) ∧	dingham, Essex)		angler, n. 1630, ob. 1687.	of Owthorpe, ob. 1669; ux

Katharine Cotton, n. 1664, = Sir Berkeley Lucy, of Brox-
ob. 1740. | bourne, 3d. bt. ob. 1759, æt. 87.

Mary Lucy, = Hon. Charles Compton, yᵗ s. George,
md. 1727. | 4th Earl of Northampton, ob. 1755.

Charles Compton, 7th Earl of = Anne Somerset, d. Charles Noel,
Northants., o.s.p. m 1763. | 4th Duke of Beaufort.

1782.
Elizabeth Compton, sole child, = Geo. Au. Henry Cavendish:
md. 1782, ob. 1835. | created, 1731, Earl of Burlington;
| n. 1754, ob. 1834.

1807.
William Cavendsh, n. 1783, = Louisa, d. Cornelius O'Callaghan,
ob. 1812. | 1st Lord Lismore, ob. 1863.

1829.
William Cavendish 7th Duke of = Blanche, 4th d. George Howard,
Devonshire. n. 1808 | 6th Earl of Carlisle, ob. 1840.
∧

SIX
LOCAL WILLS

The list of wills at the Lichfield Records Office records names of established families who occupied a prominent position. The importance of their position is a reflection either of the family name or the fortune obtained over decades or even centuries. The will of R. Bacon, 14th April 1575, and J. Bacon, 5th May 1602, relate to descendants of Richard Bacon who founded the abbey in 1141. Robert Grafton, whose will is dated 18th October 1540, justifiably is believed to be from the same family as William Grafton who surrendered the abbey in 1538.

The Bothams, long established as yeoman farmers, would be considered wealthy people. The will of Thomas Botham in 1757, illustrates a successful life:

To my sons John, Thomas, Isaac and David the sum of fourteen pounds and ten shillings each to be paid from my stocks from my farm and personal estate. To my eldest son John Botham, the house and land known as the Kidding (which I bought from Mr. Hyatt) and land at Alveston (under the Duke of Shrewsbury). To Isaac a house and croft at Denston commonly called the Meece and also land known as Rocester Field. Also to Isaac my stock and personal estate of my Rocester farm. Executor Thomas Biddulph of Abbots Clownholme.

If the poor of Rocester might envy the lifestyle of tradesmen and yeoman farmers, they would have been astounded by the wealth of Sir William Trentham whose will is dated 12th April 1633. Sir William was a direct descendant of the Trenthams who obtained the demesne land from the abbey shortly after the Dissolution of 1538. The distribution of Sir William's wealth required four pages of script and a total of 175 entries to account for the grand total of £650-11-00, a huge sum at the time. Compare the sum with the cost of building the bridge over the River Churnet or the rents listed for Lady Day in 1770 and the wealth of the Trenthams seems vast indeed.

The Lodge Entrance to Crakemarsh Hall.

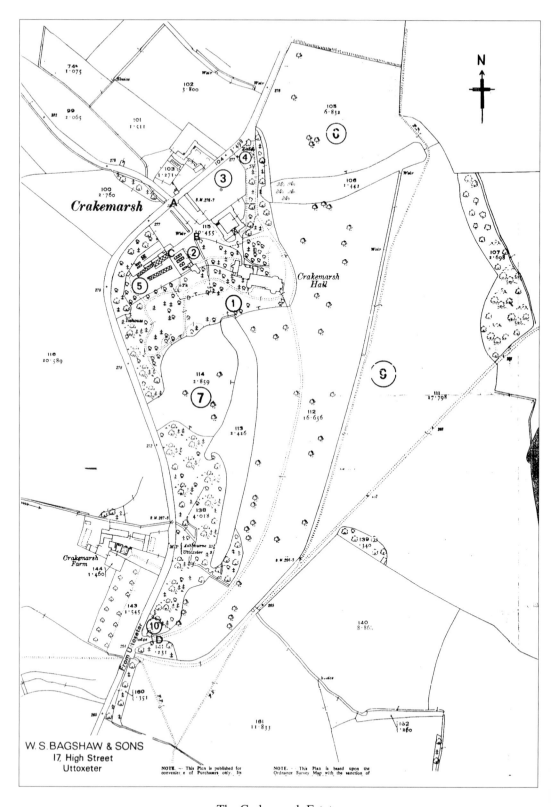

The Crakemarsh Estate

SEVEN
LORDS OF THE MANOR AND LOCAL HOUSES

The pedigree of the Trenthams of Rocester illustrates the inter marriage of the gentry. The name of Trentham became obsolete when Elizabeth Trentham married Brian Cockayne, Viscount Cullen. The couple were without issue. An earlier female line commences with Katherine Trentham marrying Sir John Stanhope. From that union emerge the familiar name of Charles Cotton, the friend of Isaac Walton, and the Cavendish family of Chatsworth. The spread of the family's influence into other local villages and estates is really beyond this book's remit, but Doveridge was already under the influence of William Cavendish in 1538 and Eaton Dovedale, nestling unobtrusively between Rocester and Doveridge, was home to the St. Pierres who relate to the Milwards and to Charles Cotton. The landed gentry hung on to a life of wealth and privilege for a thousand years. It was to take an industrial revolution, and massive educational and social reform to bring about a more equal society.

The link between Henry de Stafford and Richard Bacon is not apparent. As a nephew of Ranulph, Earl of Chester, Richard was a powerful representative of a noble family. With the exception of the king, the Earls of Chester were the most powerful family in England. In return for their continued allegiance to the Crown, the king added large tracts of land to the Earldom's already substantial holdings. During the 12th century virtually all of central England was granted to the Earls of Chester. Other Earls remained powerful, but in reality they were subservient to Chester.

The Staffords lost Rocester to Richard Bacon who in turn granted the manor to the new Augustinian monastery. After the monks were dispossessed at the Dissolution the manor passed briefly to Edward Draycott who was granted a lease for 21 years (1540) in return for a yearly rent of £38. 8s.10d. A reversion saw the manor pass to Richard Trentham, to be held in capite by Knight Service rendering £3. 8s.0d per annum. The Trentham pedigree fails to show that the manor was already being sold piece by piece before their line became extinct. In 1674 various farms were sold by Lord Cullen and his mortgagees to William Bainbrigge and others. In 1678 the mortgage of the remainder was transferred to Jeffrey and Samuel Howland. A few years later, in 1684, there was a conveyance from Lord and Lady Cullen and the Howlands to William Nabbs Esq. of Stafford.

The tithe rights followed a separate route. In 1546 Henry VIII granted the issue and profits of the tithes of hay of three farms to James Gunter and Henry Westcote, in full. In 1608, James 1st granted all the tithes of grain and hay and all other tithes belonging to the late monastery of Rocester to Simon Wiseman and Richard Moore in fee of a yearly payment of £8.13s.9d to the King and a yearly stipend of £3. 6s.8d to the curates of Rocester and Bradley.

Towards the end of 1607, Wiseman and Moore conveyed the tithes to Robert Meverell of Throwley. Robert married Elizabeth, daughter of Sir Thomas

Fleminge, Lord Chief Justice of England. The daughter of Robert and Elizabeth married Thomas, Lord Cromwell, who was later created Earl of Ardglass. Their son, Wingfield, eventually succeeded as Lord Cromwell. In 1656, Wingfield, Lord Cromwell, conveyed the tithes to Rowland Cotton of Crakemarsh and William Nabbs of Stafford. In 1665 Rowland Cotton released his interest in the tithes to William Nabbs. Once again manor and tithes were in the possession of one man.

Thus we have a line of succession for the Lord of the Manor which fluctuates with the fortunes of the Trenthams and the financial desires of the Crown.

William I - Robert de Stafford - Richard Bacon -
- The Monastery - Edward Draycot - Richard Trentham

William Nabbs had one son, Thomas who died without issue, and four daughters, Theophila who remained unmarried, Mary, Felicia and Elizabeth. Elizabeth married Robert Basville and their only daughter, Ann, became sole owner in 1733 of the manor and tithes of Rocester. In 1738 Ann married George Hunt but had no children. Mrs Ann Hunt conveyed certain tithes for a sum of £2500 to Martin Tomkinson of Nantwich in 1769. Tomkinson vested the tithes in Mr Thomas W. Orme.

In 1771 Ann Hunt devised her estates to Sarah Yarnold who married John Harvey in 1773. By marriage settlement the property was vested in Ralph Weston and James Farquharson in trust for sale. In 1778 the churchyard and the advowson of memorial rites and certain tithes were sold to Thomas Bainbrigge Esq. who conveyed them to his brother. (Ref. Staffordshire Parish Register)

Bainbrigge was, no doubt, a descendant of the family who owned the cotton mills. The Bainbrigges originated in Lockington in Leicestershire. Thomas, 1714-1798, built Woodseat in 1765 which in turn became the residence of J. F. Campbell. In 1862 the manor and advowson was purchased by Thomas Minton Campbell Esq. and his son J. F. Campbell Esq. Minton Campbell was instrumental in the demolition of the old church and the financing and building of the present church.

With the passing of Minton Campbell and the dispersion of the family estate the final ties with the manorial system and tithe rents all but disappeared.

Local Houses

Many of the substantial houses that graced the village are sadly no more. Brief references in county histories remind us of the fall from grace of even the most eminent family. The Bacons, proud descendants of the Earls of Chester, became landowners and farmers.

Richardus Trentham moved into the Abbey House after the dissolution and it remained the family seat until 1666. It was obviously in a state of decay and was probably demolished. Pitt, in his *History of Staffordshire*, reaches a similar conclusion: *"It was held by his descendants in the 17th century, but not a vestige of it now remains!"* Reference is also made to Rocester Hall being on the site of the abbey. More than likely the houses are one and the same, especially when Rocester Hall is said to have become derelict in the mid 1600s.

The Trenthams seem to have been keen gardeners and references to an Italianate garden and Queen Julian's bower feed the imagination, but it is difficult to agree with those who claim that aerial views of Abbey Field show the garden.

Pitt also refers to Mince Pie Hall, a curious mansion situated on an eminence with a turret and observatory. Mince Pie Hall, so called because of the unique styling of its roof, was more accurately known as Banks Farm. The Hall was built by the Bainbrigge family as the main residence of the Woodseat estate but was replaced after only a few years by Woodseat Hall. The Campbells, who followed the Bainbrigges into Woodseat, added two wings and also spent considerable amounts of money on improvements. They remained there until the early 1940s. The estate was finally broken up and sold on September 17th, 1941.

Crakemarsh Hall

Crakemarsh Hall occupied an attractive site on meadow land to the south of Rocester. Erdeswicke called the area Crakesmere and prior to 1066 it was part of the demesne of Algar, Earl of Mercia. William granted it to Henry de Ferrers who also owned Eaton and Doveridge. A descendant, Robert de Ferrers gave Crakemarsh to his daughter Maud on her marriage to Bertram de Verdon. The estate passed through the hands of various families. From Lord Burghersh it passed to the Delves, from the Delves to the Sheffields. The Sheffields sold it to Gilbert Collier and Gilbert's son sold it to Sir Gilbert Gerard, Master of the Rolls.

Crakemarsh Hall

Crakemarsh remained with the Gerards for several generations before passing to the Cottons who enter into the Trentham pedigree in about 1658. Elizabeth, daughter of William Cotton Esq. of Crakemarsh, married in 1774, Thomas Sheppard of Bedfordshire. Thomas was created a baronet in 1809 and on his death in 1821 was succeeded in his title by his son Sir Thomas Cotton Sheppard, Baronet. Redfern, in his *History of Uttoxeter* refers to a Lady Cotton Sheppard who was related through marriage to the Hart family of Uttoxeter.

Auction 1968
W. S. Bagshaw & Sons

Knight, Frank & Rutley

By direction of the Public Trustee

Staffordshire - Derbyshire Border   Uttoxeter 2 miles. Stoke on Trent 16 miles. Derby 19 miles.

The Crakemarsh Hall Estate including Crakemarsh Hall, A Georgian Mansion at present divided into a Principle Residence and seven flats.

Two Lodges.	Two flats in Stable Block.
Boffey Cottage.	Garden Cottage. Bungalow Yard Cottage
Fishing in the River Dove	
9 acres let	

In all 87 acres
To be offered for Sale by Auction as a whole or in ten lots.

Assessments and Outgoings.

Rateable Values.

Let 1 Crakemarsh Hall		£106	
Flat 1 Unoccupied		£ 94	
Flat 2		£ 46	
Flat 3		£ 86	
Flat 4 Unoccupied		£ 62	
Flat 5		£ 82	
Flat 6 Unoccupied		£ 50	
Flat 7 Unoccupied		£ 82	
Lot 2 Garden Cottage Unoccupied		£ 61	
Lot 3	Upper Stable Flat Unoccupied		£ 23
	Lower Stable Flat Unoccupied	£ 28	
	Boffet Cottage	£ 32	
Lot 4	North Lodge		£ 23
Lot 10	South Lodge Unoccupied		£ 19

The rate in the £ for current year is 11s-1d
Water Rate 1s-3d in the £ with a minimum of £3

Sporting

Hunting with both the North Staffordshire and the Meynell Packs.
Golf at Burton on Trent, Stoke on Trent and Ashbourne.
Racing at Uttoxeter, Wolverhampton and Nottingham.
Fishing on the River Dove which borders the property.
Rough Shooting over the property is in hand.

Lot 1	Crakemarsh Hall	5.885 acres
Lot 2	The Garden House	0.748 acres
Lot 3	Stable Block	1.817 acres
Lot 4	North Lodge	0.155 acres
Lot 5	A Walled Garden	1.85 acres
Lot 6	A Pasture Field	6.832 acres
Lot 7	A Meadow	2.859 acres
Lot 8	Fishing Rights	2.573 acres
Lot 9	An area of Parkland	64.276 acres
Lot 10	The South Lodge	0.144 acres
	Total	87.139 acres

The only daughter of Mr Hart Esq., Banker of Thornley Hall, Elizabeth Maria Margaret, was married to the Honourable Richard Cavendish in 1841. The union of the Harts and the Cavendish heirs brought about the succession of the family estate and the extension of the family name to Hart Cavendish.

The estate remained in the care of the Cavendish family until the death of Tyrell William Cavendish in about 1967. The name Tyrell is of significance for several reasons. The Harts are said to have descended from the Tyrells and a Mary Tyrell, daughter of Elizabeth Usher, married Henry Cavendish.

In 1968 the Crakemarsh estate was put up for auction by Bagshaws of Uttoxeter and Knight, Frank and Rutley. In all 87 acres were auctioned in ten lots. The Hall itself is described as a Georgian mansion although its origins are less precise. A picture in 1912 states that the Hall and its two polygonal bays were built in the early 1800s on the site of a much older house. There is also reference to the 'sumptuous' 17th century staircase that had been removed from another house and incorporated into the Hall. A detailed description appears in the catalogue:

The first floor is approached by a magnificent staircase in three flights. It has a moulded handrail with carved banisters and newel posts with acorn finials. It is almost certainly the work of Grinling Gibbons, the wood carver to George I and Sir Christopher Wren, and incorporates his usual sign of a peacock on the landing. If so, it is one of only two or three remaining.

Whether the auction was successful is debatable. JCB purchased the estate for £89,000 in 1972 with the intention of turning it into the company training centre. However, this plan was abandoned and the estate was sold again in 1976.

A fire in 1983 virtually gutted the place, causing it to be demolished. A few ruins and estate buildings remained for a while until the site of the Hall was sold again in 1999 - this time for building land. During the ownership by JCB much of the contents of the house were removed. The Grinling Gibbons staircase is thought to have been despatched to America and incorporated into the home of Sir Anthony and Lady Bamford.

Tom Harrison, Sam Patterson and Joseph Arnold Harrison, who worked at Barrow Hill.
See chapter 15, Paul Harrison.

Staff at Barrow Hill Hall.

Barrow Hill

Situated on a hill to the north of Rocester, Barrow Hill is aptly named. The site may well have been a hill fort in the iron age and the discovery of iron age relics would support such thoughts. Redfern, in his *History of Uttoxeter*, also refers to Barrow Hill. His comments are unconfirmed but worthy of mention: *A field at the entrance of Rocester from Barrow Hill, is named Lyggets, from the Saxon word Lyd which means to cover or protect.* It is further suggested that there was a strong gate across the road entering Rocester, at which there was a nightly watch. Barrow Hill House occupied the site and was the home of Mr. and Mrs White before being purchased by Captain Henry Dawson. When he returned home from the Boer war in 1900 with an amputated leg he was afforded a hero's return, with the streets decorated. On his arrival, the villagers took the horse from the carriage shafts at the railway station and pulled him home in the carriage, preceded by the village brass band.

In more recent times Barrow Hill was used as a horticultural nursery and later by JCB as a club and restaurant before becoming a nursing home.

By Instructions from
The Honble. Mrs. DAWSON and Major A. F. DAWSON.

Barrow Hill : Rocester.

4 miles from Uttoxeter.
The Uttoxeter to Ashbourne Bus passes the Entrance.

Catalogue of a Portion
OF THE
Antique and Modern Furnishings

and OUTDOOR EFFECTS

which will be SOLD BY AUCTION on

Thursday, July 16th, 1942,
BY
W. S. BAGSHAW & SONS.

SALE at 11 o'clock prompt.
ON VIEW by Catalogue, 6d. each,
to admit Two Persons on TUESDAY,
July 14th, 11 to 4 o'clock.

The catalogue for the dispersal sale of Barrow Hill in 1942.

Below: Barrow Hill c.1900

Catalogue.

—:::—

Thursday, July 16th, 1942,
: at 11 o'clock prompt. :

—:::—

GLASS.

LOT
1 Twelve Double-lipped Finger Bowls
2 Frosted Glass Jug and 4 Goblets
3 Five Water Bottles and 2 Small Decanters
4 Two Cut-glass Claret Jugs and 2 Decanters
5 Thirteen Green Claret Glasses
6 Five Green Wine Glasses and 5 various Wine Glasses
7 Four Glass Vases
8 Pair of Venetian Decanters
9 Sundry Glass

CHINA.

10 Pair of Continental China Figure Candlesticks, 12" high, and Pair of White Dresden China Vases
11 Minton China Vase, Minton Majolica Jug, and Wedgwood Basalt Bowl
12 Nine various Oriental Plates and Circular Dishes
13 Pair of Nankin China Plaques, 14" diameter, and 3 ditto, 14", blue decoration
14 Pair of Oriental China Saucer-shaped Dishes, 15" diameter, blue decoration

—4—

LOT
15 Pair of China Vases encrusted flowers, and Minton China Rose Bowl
16 Wedgwood Jasper Copy of the Portland Vase
17 Part Oriental China Tea and Coffee Service, 37 pieces
18 Angouleme China Dessert Service, 49 pieces, cornflower and spring decoration
19 White China Basket pattern Dessert Service, 18 pieces
20 Dresden China Tea and Coffee Service, 19 pieces
21 Ten China Coffee Cups and Saucers
22 Five White and Gold Coffee Cups and Saucers
23 China Coffee Set, blue and gilt band
24 Three Oriental Pottery Jardinieres, and 3 Continental Pottery Figures
25 Twelve various Oriental Plates, and 4 Oriental China Bowls
26 Eight Oriental China Pots and Covers, 5 Oriental China Cups and Saucers, and 6 Oriental China Saucers
27 Seven various Blue Printed Cups, and 3 Small Bowls
28 Fourteen Soup Plates, 2 Meat Plates, and 4 Nursery Plates printed ducks
29 Fourteen pieces Dinner Ware
30 Eleven Soup Plates
31 Twenty China Tea Plates
32 Lustre Jug, 2 Minton Ornaments, etc.

—5—

CONDITIONS OF SALE.

1. The highest bidder shall be the purchaser, and if any dispute arise between two or more bidders, the Lot in question shall be put up again and re-sold.

2. All Lots shall be taken to with all faults and errors of description whatsoever, and no guarantee is given as to the genuineness, quality, number or measurements of the Lots, but every care has been taken in compiling the Catalogue. The Purchase Money shall be paid at any time during the progress of the Sale when demanded by the Auctioneers or their Clerk.

3. Each Lot after being knocked down shall be considered as delivered to the purchaser thereof, and the Auctioneers will not, neither will any person in their employ hold themselves responsible for the safety of such Lot.

4. No Lot shall be removed from the place of Sale under any pretence whatever until paid for.

5. Upon any purchaser failing to comply with these Conditions, the Lot or Lots bought by him shall be re-sold by Public Auction or Private Treaty, and any expense incurred, or deficiency arising from such re-sale, shall be made good by the defaulter at the present Sale.

6. The Auctioneers reserve the right to alter, re-arrange, or withdraw any Lots if necessary from Sale.

7. Should any question arise not provided for in the foregoing Conditions, the decision of the Auctioneers shall be final.

8. Strangers paying by Cheque will be expected to produce their Banker's or other References.

LASTLY.—The Auctions Bidding Agreement Act, 1927.

Auctioneers :
W. S. BAGSHAW & SONS, F.A.I.
Uttoxeter : Ashbourne : Bakewell : Derby.

NOTES.

Intending Purchasers are particularly requested to note Lots marked * when viewing, as they will not be removed from their respective rooms on the day of Sale, but sold in Catalogue order.

On No Account can any Lot or Lots be delivered during the hours of the Sale, but may be cleared immediately after the Sale.

Any Damage caused by removing the Lots must be made good by the Purchaser thereof.

A Caterer will be in attendance.

On View by Catalogue, 6d. each, to admit two persons, on Tuesday, July 14th, from 11 to 4 o'clock.

The Sale will be held in a Marquee and commence at 11 o'clock prompt.

LOT
33 Sundry China
34 Ditto
35 Ditto
36
37

SILVER and PLATE.

38 Pair of 8" Silver Fruit Dishes with pierced borders
39 Silver 7" Salver with raised border
40 Silver Boat-shaped Inkstand with pierced and gadroon border
41 Silver Inkstand with 2 Containers and pierced gallery border
42 Plain Silver Boat-shaped Inkstand, one Container
43 Pair of Silver Corinthian Column Candlesticks, 9" high
44 Silver Sweetmeat Dish, Cream Jug, and Small Sugar Bowl
45 Small Geo. III. Silver Pap Boat
46 Victorian Silver Beaker and Embossed Silver Muffineer
47 Silver Mustard Pot and 2 Silver Peppers
48 Cut-glass Claret Jug, Silver mounts
49 Pair of Plated Candlesticks, 7½" high
50 An Oriental Plated Cabaret Set, 10 pieces
51 Tortoishell Paper Knife, silver handle; Indian Silver Sugar Bowl: Sheffield Plate Snuffer Tray
52 Case of 6 Fish Knives and Forks and Pair of Servers

—6—

LOT
53 E.P. Engraved Hot-water Jug
54 Large Plated Well Dish and Cover
55 Three Sheffield Plate Chamber Candlesticks and Snuffers
56 Two Pewter Tankards, one Oak ditto, and one Beaker
57 Pair Sheffield Plate Candlesticks, 9" high
58 E.P. Teapot and E.P. Hot-water Jug (lid missing)
59 E.P. Oval Butter Dish and Cover, and E.P. Butter Dish Stand and Cover
60 E.P. Mustard Pot; Glass Mustard, Silver top; and 2 Small Peppers
61 Crumb Scoop, Ivory handle
62 Two E.P. Sauce Boats and S.P. Snuffer Tray
63 Pair of S.P. Candlesticks, 7½" high
64 E.P. Oval Tray, 30", raised border
65 Twelve Fish Knives
66 E.P. Egg Stand
67 Oak Biscuit Barrel, E.P. mounts
68
69
70

ENTRANCE HALL.

71 Two Mounted Heads
72 Two   ditto
73 Two   ditto and Crocodile Head
74 Four various Engravings in black frames

—7—

LOT
75 Square Oak Two-tier Table on turned legs
76 Oak Pedestal Stand
77 Oriental China Umbrella Stand
78 Pair of Carved Mahogany Hall Chairs
79 Black Wool Rug
80
81

MORNING ROOM.

82 Six various Framed Engravings
83 Pair of Mezzotint Engravings, Rev. and Mrs. Granville
84 Copper Embossed Jardiniere
85 Pair of Brass Embossed 2-Light Wall Sconces
86 Old Copper Warming Pan (damaged)
87 Oblong Bevel-plate Frameless Wall Mirror
88 Carved Oak Chest, 3' 3"
89 Massive Carved Oak and Inlaid Armchair
90 Mahogany Extending Dining Table with 4 extra leaves and leaf cabinet
91 Quantity of old Military Uniforms
92 Wilton Pile Carpet, 17' × 13' 6"
93 Maroon Felt Curtain, embroidered floral border
94
95

DINING ROOM.

96 Pewter Jardiniere
97 Pair of Engravings, Highland Scenes, by Peter Graham, green and gilt frames

—8—

LOT
172 Cast Fender and Brass Fire Implements
173
174

STAIRCASE and LANDING.

175 Four Engravings in gilt frames
176 Three Sets of Antlers
177 Case of Butterflies and Moths
178 Glazed Case of South American Birds on Rosewood Table Stand
179
180

BEDROOM No. 1.

181 Chimney Mirror in white painted frame
182 Light Oak Sutherland Table
183 Child's Tall Chair
184 Deal Pembroke Table
185 Pair of Large Tapestry Curtains
186 Two Chairs, rush seats

BEDROOM No. 2.

187 Chimney Mirror in Oak frame
188 Pair of Mahogany Toilet Tables
189 Mahogany Pedestal Cupboard
190 Mahogany Bed Steps
191 Four-fold Screen
192 *Gent.'s Mahogany Wardrobe, fitted 5 sliding trays above, enclosed by pair of panelled doors, and 4 drawers below

—13—

LOT
193 Four Chairs, cane seats
194 Cast Fender and Fire Implements
195 Pair of Plush Curtains'
196
197

BEDROOM No. 3.

198 Various Pictures
199 Walnut Tripod Table
200 Oak Writing Table, fitted 3 drawers, carved fronts
201 Mahogany Toilet Table
202 Stuff-over Armchair, loose cretonne cover
203 *Mahogany Breakfront Wardrobe, 8', fitted 2 hanging compartments, 4 drawers and 4 sliding trays
204 Mahogany 4-post Bedstead, cretonne hangings, Box Spring Mattress, Hair Mattress
205 Mahogany Bed Steps
206 Axminster Carpet, 18' × 14'
207 Antique Brass Pierced Fender
208

BEDROOM No. 4.

209 Sundry Ornaments
210 Sundry Pictures
211 Mahogany Toilet Table
212 Odd Toilet Ware
213 Mahogany Swing-frame Toilet Mirror

—14—

LOT
214 Low Easy Chair, seat and back upholstered needlework
215 Mahogany Inlaid Chest of 5 drawers
216 Stuff-over Armchair, loose cretonne cover
217 *Mahogany Wardrobe, 6' 3" wide, fitted hanging compartment, 4 sliding trays and 4 drawers
218 *Brass-mounted Bedstead, 5', Wire Mattress, Wool Bed, Hair Mattress
219 Box Ottoman
220 Four Blankets
221 Four ditto
222 Four ditto
223 Four ditto
224 Five ditto
225 Two Eiderdowns
226 Wilton Pile Carpet, 17' × 10' 6"
227
228

BEDROOM No. 5.

229 Various Pictures
230 Chimney Mirror in white painted frame
231 Mahogany Kneehole Dressing Table, fitted 9 drawers
232 Pair of Mahogany Toilet Tables
233 Mahogany Swing-frame Toilet Mirror
234 Two Birch Frame Chairs
235 All-Brass Curb
236
237

—15—

BEDROOM No. 7.

LOT
238 Pair of Brass Candlesticks
239 Two Cases of Birds
240 Walnut Oval 2-tier Washstand and Toilet Ware
241 Sheraton Mahogany Inlaid Swing-frame Toilet Mirror
242 Mahogany Chest of 4 drawers
243 Pair of Blue Lined Casement Cloth Curtains and Valance

BEDROOM No. 8.

244 Walnut 2-tier Table
245 Mahogany Pedestal Cupboard
246 Mahogany Toilet Table
247 Toilet Ware
248 Grained Deal Hanging Wardrobe, 3' 6"
249 Strip of Axminster Carpet
250 Pair of Green Lined Casement Cloth Curtains
251 Brass-bound Wire Fire Guard
252
253

BEDROOM No. 9.

254 Various Pictures
255 Sundry Curtains
256 Ditto
257 Pair of Painted Toilet Tables
258 Pair ditto

—16—

LOT
259 Two Nests of Shelves
260 Box Ottoman
261 Ditto
262 Antique Sheraton Mahogany Inlaid Enclosed Washstand
263 Mahogany Swing-frame Toilet Mirror
264 *Oak Breakfront Housekeeper's Cupboard, 7', fitted 3 cupboards above, enclosed by panelled doors, and 4 drawers and 2 cupboards below
265 *Brass-mounted Bedstead, 5', Heal Box Spring Mattress, Wool Bed, Feather Bolster
266 Feather Bed and Bolster

BEDROOM No. 10.

267 Walnut Octagonal Table
268 Oak Chest of 5 drawers
269 Painted Toilet Table and Towel Rail
270 Mahogany Swing-frame Toilet Mirror
271 *Brass-mounted Bedstead, 3' 6", Two Wool Mattresses, Feather Bolster and Pillow
272 Wilton Pile Carpet, 16' × 10' 6"
273
274

BATH ROOM.

275 Painted Toilet Table, Linen Basket and Towel Rail
276 Deal Table, 5' 9" × 3'

—17—

LOT
277 Pair of Blue Lined Casement Cloth Curtains
278
279

TOP FLOOR.

280 Pair of Mahogany Bed Posts
281 Painted Cupboard, 5' 6" wide
282 Painted Wardrobe, 5', fitted hanging compartment and 4 drawers

MAIDS' SITTING ROOM.

283 Various Pictures
284 Two-tier Circular Table
285 Oak Oval Tripod Table
286 Mahogany-frame Reclining Chair, cane back
287 Couch, upholstered printed cretonne
288 Stuff - over Armchair, upholstered printed cretonne
289 Strip of Wilton Carpet and Cast Fender
290 Hip Bath and Book Shelves
291 Old Gramophone
292 Various Bird Cages
293 Walnut Stationery Cabinet
294

BUTLER'S PANTRY.

295 Sundry Trays
296 Mahogany Butler's Tray
297 Oak Butler's Tray and Stand

—18—

LOT
298 Deal Table, 6' × 3'
299 Sundry Crockery
300 Ditto

KITCHEN.

301 Deal Table, 8' × 3' 4"
302 Set of 3 Steps
303 Electric Iron
304 Brass Maslin Kettle

SCULLERY.

305 Deal Table, 4' 3" × 2' 8"
306 Deal Table, 4' 8" × 2' 6"

LAUNDRY.

307 Deal Table, 12' × 3' 6"
308 Ironing Stove and Piping

WASH-HOUSE.

309 Deal Table
310 Old Ice Box
311 Box Form

CONSERVATORY.

312 Two Palms in pots
313 Various Aspidistras in pots
314 Begonias in pots
315 Various Plants in pots
316 Ditto

—19—

OUTSIDE EFFECTS.

LOT
317 Six Garden Chairs
318 Garden Seat
319 Various Sun Blinds
320 Deal Cupboard
321 Ditto
322 Chick Hoover
323 Ditto
324 Chick Troughs
325 Pair of Stone Garden Vases
326 Pair ditto
327 Pair ditto
328 One Large Stone Vase
329 Ladder, 48 rounds
330

Doveleys

A little further north lies Doveleys. Doveleys was built, by the Heywood family who were bankers from Duffield in Derbyshire in about 1839, and was the home of Sir Thomas Percival Heywood and Lady Hilda Margaret Heywood. The house was burnt down in 1873 and rebuilt exactly as before. A house was already in existence prior to 1839 as can be seen from the entry for 1834 in White's Gazetteer. It records Benjamin Heywood and a bailiff, Thomas Wilson, as living at Doveleys. The Heywoods were considered great benefactors to Denstone.

The house was occupied as an extension to Abbotsholme School between 1947 and 1953, and was then purchased by the local authority who converted it into a reform school. Towards the end of the 20th century the house and estate were disposed of by the county council to a Uttoxeter businessman, Mr M. Barrett. Mr Barrett has plans for development which include the building of houses, the conversion of Doveleys probably into a hotel, and the creation of a garden centre.

Clownholme

Clownholme, to the east of the village, is more in Eaton Dovedale than Rocester, although geographically part of Rocester. The same can be said of Monksclownholme. Historically Clownholme is closely connected with the abbey at Rocester and there is the suggestion of connecting tunnels between the house and the monastery. Clownholme has remained mostly unchanged for over a hundred years although in 1874 William Webb incorporated two houses into a single larger dwelling. As an aside it is thought that Mary Anne Evans (George Eliot) was a regular visitor to Clownholme during her time at Ellastone. The carvings on the timbered gable ends are similar to others in Ellastone and are attributed her carpenter father on whom Mary based the character Adam Bede.

The Webb family have long been associated with Clownholme. Documents in the possession of Miss Lydia Clarke, of Clownholme Cottages, show that the family farmed the land and lived at Clownholme in the 18th Century. An unusual aspect of the family is the lack of male heirs. A son, William, was born in the 19th century but died at the age of twelve and succession reverted once again to the female line. The female line remained strong and many of the ladies retained the name Webb even after marriage. The ownership of Clownholme passed to Lydia Clarke, a direct descendant of the Webb family and probably the last to bear the name Lydia, a name which also passed through the generations. Miss Clarke leased Clownholme to Abbotsholme school on a permanent basis on condition that it was maintained in its original state. Tradition has it that Mr. Lyons of Tutbury Hall lived for some time at Clownholme.

Abbotsholme, the public school, was formally Abbots Clownholme. Records exist from around 1700 and a former resident of Monksclownholme, Mrs Appleby, indicated deeds showing a new wing being added to the house in 1725, a fact borne out by the change in architectural style. Abbotsholme had been enlarged and altered over the years and now bears little resemblance to the original building.

Woodseat Hall [A record of unknown origin from an article by Marilyn Oxley]

Woodseat Hall was built in 1767 by Thomas Bainbrigge, who was born in 1714. He also purchased the Manor of Rocester in 1778. In 1750, as Sheriff for the County of Derbyshire, it was his duty to proclaim George III on his accession to the throne. Thomas died in 1798 and is buried at Rocester.

His son, also Thomas, was born in 1751 and lived all his life at Woodseat. At his death in 1818 he left his estates at Woodseat, Rocester and Derby to his daughter.

Woodseat was probably last used in the 1920's, after which it fell into decay•. The site was purchased in the early 1940's by Albert Nash, a well-known landscape designer and nurseryman from Uttoxeter. He and his staff restored fourteen acres of gardens plus the original greenhouses and conservatories, and for some years the Hall flourished as a market garden and nursery.

The family tree is also from Marilyn Oxley's article

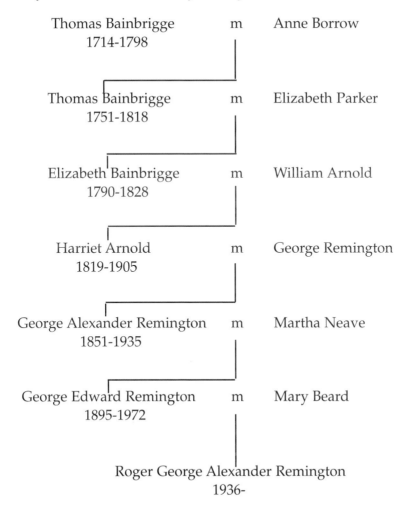

Thomas Bainbrigge   m   Anne Borrow
1714-1798

Thomas Bainbrigge   m   Elizabeth Parker
1751-1818

Elizabeth Bainbrigge   m   William Arnold
1790-1828

Harriet Arnold   m   George Remington
1819-1905

George Alexander Remington   m   Martha Neave
1851-1935

George Edward Remington   m   Mary Beard
1895-1972

Roger George Alexander Remington
1936-

Also of unknown origin, is the following extract from a diary of Thomas Bainbrigge.**

Diary of Thomas Bainbrigge (1751-1818)

Sept 13th. 1804
    Rode to Farley the day appointed for the sale of Lord
    Shrewsbury's cottages etc. £574.10.00

Sept 19th. 1804
    Returned to Woodseat in evening - called on Lord
    Vernon afterwards on commissions at Eyland Lodge
    about my allotment.

Sept 26th 1804
    Went in chariot to Stallington

Sept 29th 1804
    I dined with Mr. J. Hope, the Mayor, at the George.

Oct 17th 1804
    Sally Gaunt came. Hired her for 51 weeks at £5.50

Oct 18th 1804
    Fieldhouse left - behaved ill, will have him no more

Oct 19th 1804
    Run 3 hares, more killed - dogs bad

Oct 23rd 1804
    Rode Chestnut Mare to Mrs May's sale - dined and slept.
    Bought a 3 year old cow for £9.5.0

Oct 24th 1804
    Blagg, Jack and I drove the cow home.

Dec 13th 1804
    Planted the litch with apple trees from Hammond of
    Rudgeley. 2 Golden Pippins - one set in Woodseat garden.

---

* A brother of the second Thomas Bainbrigge, Joseph, contested a will written in favour of Elizabeth Bainbrigge. The legal costs of the case were so high that Woodseat was eventually sold to raise money. The property was never inherited by the Arnolds or the Remingtons.

** My thanks to Mr. S. Glover.

EIGHT
A WORKING VILLAGE

In Rocester we are aware of Neolithic man and his ancient crafts, and later the Romans, a trading nation in every sense of the word. Most villages had a single mill powered by a water wheel; Rocester had corn grinding mills on the River Churnet and also on the River Dove. There may well have been more than one mill on the Dove, because the site, now occupied by the semi derelict Cotton Mill, is extensive and well planned.

As the River Dove entered the village, a mill race diverted the flow of water into a powerful force along its confined channel, to turn the traditional wheel. Its mechanism transferred the water power to the grinding pan into which the grain was poured. To control the river and the vagaries of the weather, a weir and a dam held large volumes of water on standby to ensure continuity of supply. The system, primitive by today's standards, served its purpose very well.

The monks from the nearby abbey were equally productive. Apart from the growing of fruit and vegetables, and of course their religious endowments, wool was their main source of income. The monastery had large flocks of sheep and reference is made to a fulling mill, a process in which the cloth was enhanced in its thickness. The art of the fuller has long gone although fullers' earth is still in use in other trades.

The industrial revolution brought dramatic changes to the social and economic life of Britain - and Rocester. Cottage industries, from nailmaking to cotton spinning, were limited by the speed of the worker and demand often outstripped supply. The introduction of the factory system, even in its crudest form, enabled mass production to meet the demand in this country and overseas. The production of iron in Coalbrookdale is an obvious example. Equally important was the introduction of cotton machinery. Cotton spinning was to be of immense benefit to Rocester and, in some ways, was a natural progression from the wool trade enjoyed by the monks a few centuries before.

When cotton spinning was introduced to Rocester it came from one of the giants of industry. Richard Arkwright was born in Preston in 1732 and was the son of a tailor. His initial profession was that of peruke (wig) maker, and he spent much of his time wandering the countryside buying hair and working as a barber. His mind was evidently elsewhere; he spent his time deep in thought on ways to improve his fortune. He worked with Thomas Highs and John Kay who had experimented with spinning machines, and in 1768 Arkwright joined with John Kay and rented premises in Preston where they perfected a roller spinning machine. From the roller spinning machine emerged the spinning frame and then the water frame.

Arkwright was confident that the water frame would meet all expectations but he lacked the funds to patent his machine. So he went into partnership with

Corn Mill and Churnet Bridge.

Church Street, Rocester.

Whites Gazetteer, 1851

Allenby, David. — Coal Dealer
Alsop, Thomas. — Surgeon
Baddeley, Whieldon. — Solicitor
Barkes, John. — Plumber and Painter
Carter, Joseph. 11 — Saddler
Gerrard, George. — Corn Miller
Heywood, Thomas Percival Esq. Doveleys
Hollins, Henry. — Stone Engraver
Hooper, George. — Coal Dealer
Horden, Joseph. — Brick Maker
Houldsworth, Thos. Esq. MP Lace manufacturer
Kemp, Thomas. — Horse Breaker
Leadbeater, James. — Book Keeper
Leadbeater, Thomas. — Warehouseman
Meakin, James. — Book Keeper
Miller, Robert. — Goods Clerk
Palmby, Fras. D. — Solicitor
Pendlebury, Fras. 10 — Station Master
Sheldon, Edw. — Joiner and Sheriff's Officer
Stoncer, Richard. — Bricklayer
Sumners, Henry. — Schoolmaster
Sutcliffe, Rev. Jno (bapt) Schoolmaster
Swayne, Thomas. James
Thomson, James. — Joiner and Parish Clerk
Walker, Ralph. — Wheelwright
Wardle, Thos. Esq. Woodseat
Wardle, William. — Bricklayer
Watson, Mr. Chas and Misses
White, Mrs. Maria. Barrow Hill
Williamson, Rev. Geo. F. — Incumbent

Inns and Taverns

Boat. 11 — John Campion
Cock. — Maria Berrisford
Cross Keys. — Mary Ann Cope
Greyhound. — Joseph Salt
Red Lion. — Elizabeth Keates
Shoulder of Mutton. — Uriah Prince

Beer Houses.
Clarke, Ann 1
Handson, Thomas
Tomlinson, Jph

Blacksmiths.
Bolt, John 5
Corden, Joseph
Shaw, James

Butchers.
Corden, John
Goodwin, John
Lawson, Thomas
Mountney, Chas
Waterall, George

Farmers   *Owners.
Alcock, Wm 6
Atkins, Wm*
Bennet, Joseph 9
Brandon, Walter 4
Berrisford, Thomas
Burton, Edward
Carnall, Wm.* 15
Cope, Samual 6
Dutton, John 6
Finney, Samuel 7
Fox, Thomas
Hainsworth, W 6
Laughton, Rd* 7
Loundes, Jph
Morris, Mary 8
Prince, George 2
Prince, Uriah 5
Selcock, Chas 3
Smith, Thomas
Tomlinson, Sl 1
Walker, Richard
Webb, William *
Wood, Thomas

Shoemakers.
Baldrey, George
Boulton, John
Gaunt, Edward
Gaunt, Wm
Jackson, Reuben
Locke, Thomas
Noakes, George
Shepley, Wm

Shopkeepers.
Alcock, Wm 6
Boulton, John
Dakin, Robert
Gerrard, George
Greaslay, Maria
Horden, Joseph. Jnr.
Hudson, Thomas
Titley, Thomas
Walker, Joseph (and Joiner)
Wooley, Joseph

Railway: Trains 4 times a day each way and a bus to Ashborne twice a day.
Carrier.: Thomas Salt To Ashbourne Tue, Thur and Sat.   To Uttoxeter Mon, Wed and Fri.

Key to numbers: Those marked:
1 reside at Aders. 2 at Banks. 3 Barrow Hill.
4 Clownham. 5 Combridge. 6 Denstone. 7 Dovecliff.
8 Quixhill. 9 Riddings. 10 Rocester Green. 11 Stubwoods.

Ashbourne Road c. 1900.

High Street c. 1900. The pub on the right is the Cross Keys.

two merchants, John Smalley and David Thornley. The patent followed in 1769 and also a move to Nottingham and the addition of two more partners who provided more finance. Frederick Strutt and Samuel Need were connected to the hosiery industry and, no doubt, provided business expertise as well as money.

It was Arkwright, however, who had the vision and the technical expertise and in 1771 he built a water-powered mill at Cromford near Matlock. Success was soon assured. He built more factories to meet the growing demand for cheap cotton cloth and the village of Rocester was the site of one of these, appropriately enough, by the River Dove, home to the millers, the flax gatherers, the fuller and other village industries of the past.

The old mills were mentioned frequently in parish records and had a chequered life. William Horsley refers to the mills in his will of 1727 when they passed to his grandson John Challoner. On John's death in 1758 they passed to his daughter Mary who later married a John West. In 1773 they were acquired by another William Horsley and from Horsley they passed to Richard Arkwright on 10th October 1781 for £820 - a substantial amount at the time.

Although corn grinding continued in the village, it was more than likely restricted to the operators of the mill on the River Churnet, after Arkwright's factory was built in 1782. Arkwright paid £412 for 1,575 square yards of adjacent fields to widen the mill race. It is believed that Arkwright's mill had two water wheels, one internal and one external, although nothing now remains. The stone arches on either side of the mill, at sluice level, probably housed the internal wheel. (Ref. 1 on the site plan). Latter day experts suggest that the two wheels would have been inadequate but such comment flies in the face of Arkwright's ability and knowledge.

More power may well have been needed when the first extension was built as a wing on the side of the original mill (Ref. 2). The new wing was built to house the engine and the winding gear that were installed to meet the growing demand for Arkwright's cotton products. The interior wheel was removed and the arches sealed, along with all openings on the eastern elevation. The original wheel at the end of the mill remained and the dam was extended to feed the two additional wheels built by Hewes in the new wing. Arkwright, it seems, was not the most patient of men, for he quickly went from project to project. Certainly he must have had great energy.

In January 1783 the mill was acquired by Richard Arkwright, Junior, for £3,000. The cost of the enterprise almost certainly exceeded this as he was also responsible for the cost of the extension. He recouped some of his investment in January 1786 when he sold a third share to Richard Bridden. The partnership continued until about 1806, when Richard Bridden acquired full ownership. Whether Arkwright remained at the mill in some capacity is conjecture, but to all intents and purposes the Arkwright connection was severed. The name remains in peoples' minds to this day although the association was for just twenty-four years.

Upon the death of Richard Bridden in 1814, his estate was willed to his eldest son Samuel. Trustees of the will were Samuel Simpson, Richard Simpson and

Joseph Bridden. Any powers remaining with Arkwright were now lost as he and Simpson renounced all advantages under the will.

When Joseph Bridden died in 1820, Richard Simpson was left as the only trustee. The Briddens appear to have had little interest in the mill until in March 1825 when Francis and John Bridden took on a long term lease and began to manage the business. They may well have taken a mortgage on the property to raise capital and their business appears to have been unsuccessful. The mill was offered for sale in 1831 and again a year later.

Staffordshire Advertiser; 23 July 1831

To Spinners, Power Loom Manufacturers, &c.
To be sold by Private Treaty, or to be let.
The Rocester Cotton Mills and Waterfalls, situated on the River Dove, close to the Canal, at nearly equal distance from Ashbourne, Cheadle and Uttoxeter; together with an excellent Dwelling-House, Offices, Out buildings, and Grounds, pleasantly situated a short distance from the Works, and fitted up for the residence of a Genteel Family; two other Dwelling Houses, and Gardens, suitable for managers or foremen; and thirty-nine Cottages; also, about one hundred and twenty acres of the richest Meadow Land, on the banks of the river and partly adjoining the house.
The Mills are good substantial brick buildings, now filled with throstle spinning machinery, all of which, or any part thereof, may be taken by the purchaser, and if let, by the tenant at a fair valuation..... The machinery is turned by three excellent water wheels, (two made by Hewes), and supplied by the whole stream of the River Dove, which at all seasons of the year produces an effective force, equal to seventy horses power, with wear (weir), floodgates, and breast work for the wheels, all substantially set in stone, and a considerable part of the heavy gearing is nearly new. - Premises having all these decided advantages for manufacturing purposes, ..., are seldom, if ever, offered to public notice...

Staffordshire Advertiser, 28 July 1832.

To be sold by auction (on 28 Aug. and following days) on the premises called Rocester Cotton Mills... The entire of the preparing and Cotton Spinning machinery in the said mills, consisting, among other things, of cotton openers, double blowers, 126 carding engines, 18 inches on the wire, mostly in new frames, well clothed and in good condition; seven new carding machines, 36 inches on the wire, 40 inch cylinders, and 20 inch doffers with drawing boxes in front, also several others of the same not complete; several of Creightons grinding machines for 18 and 36 inch cards, nine drawing frames with double heads and mostly new, three slubbing frames, 26 spindles each, and one of 30 spindles, all for 9´ inch bobbins, six roving frames of 40 spindles, two ditto ditto of 48, and one ditto of 60 spindles, all for 6 inch bobbins; the whole of these having been recently made by Cocker and Higgins. Three stretchers 78, 83 and 90 spindles, eight nearly new throstles, 96 spindles, by Gore, one ditto, 192 spindles, by Hewes, all in polished framework, nine ditto of various sizes, containing 1200 spindles, two doubling frames, 120 and 84 spindles each, 2" lift, 42 drums of water frames, 96 spindles each, most part with new spindles, flys and steps, and generally in good condition, 22 bobbin-reels, making-up press, large quantity of 2´ shafting and counter drums... Also well fitted up smithy, turners, fitters and joiners Shops...

A possible cause for the mill's failure was a lack of investment in better equipment. The mills were originally equipped with water frames suitable for spinning medium counts cotton. These served well enough during the Napoleonic Wars but became outdated afterwards. During the post-war depression, competition with Lancashire mills grew fiercer, and there was a rush to install throstles, a more modern version of the water frame. Rocester's conversion probably came too late and the sale of the mill was the inevitable result. There were no immediate takers and it was not until 16th January 1833 that Thomas Houldsworth, a Lancashire spinner, purchased the mills and paid off the mortgage.

Houldsworth was also the highest bidder at a sale held in the Cock Inn in 1836 at which extra land was purchased and added to the mill estate. The land was formally in the ownership of James Blair a beneficiary under the will of William Bainbrigge, who was declared bankrupt.

The mill appears to have been profitable for Houldsworth who retained it until his death in 1852. The addition of the main extension (Ref. 3 on site plan) may have stretched the finances of the Briddens but proved of great benefit to Houldsworth and added to the valuation of his property. At his death, his Manchester mills and his Rocester mill were valued jointly at £110,616. The property was divided among his family. His brother William received one third, a brother, Henry, $4/15$, his sister Ann Hussey, $1/15$, and a nephew, Henry, the final third. Among the trustees the names of two well-known fine spinners appear, James Murray and Mr McConnel.

The nephew, Henry Houldsworth, bought out his uncles and aunt and took over the company. Henry appears to have been a favourite of his uncle Thomas, as he and James Nicholson had already been made co-partners, although Thomas put up the money to the extent of £50,000 in his own name, £50,000 for Henry and £20,000 for James. As James did not find the original £20,000 he probably had no qualms about then selling his share to Henry for £10,000.

Henry Houldsworth turned out to be both a benefactor and a sound businessman. In an effort to consolidate his land into one lot he swapped various fields with his neighbours, one of whom was William Bainbrigge, a descendant of the Woodseat Bainbrigges. Around the same time, 1854, the houses on West View Road were built to accommodate his employees. The former name of Love Lane was no doubt considered too fanciful by the 19th century businessmen. It is worth noting that the houses on the High Street by the River Churnet were also built for the factory workers. The Houldsworths were enlightened in other ways and were responsible for the building of the village school in 1852.

In 1861 more land was acquired when, on 24th December, the sale was completed for Dove Meadows, above the iron bridge, from Mr Dawson of Barrow Hill. A little later, in September 1864, other land exchanges took place resulting in boundaries recognisable today, with the abbey fields of Mr Atkins, the churchyard and various footpaths and rights of way remaining.

Despite all Henry Houldsworth's beneficience, the same could not be said of his descendants. Henry died in 1868 and left his mill and property to his son William Henry. William's tenure was a disaster for the people of Rocester. William

Tutbury Mill.

Textile machinery in Tutbury Mill.

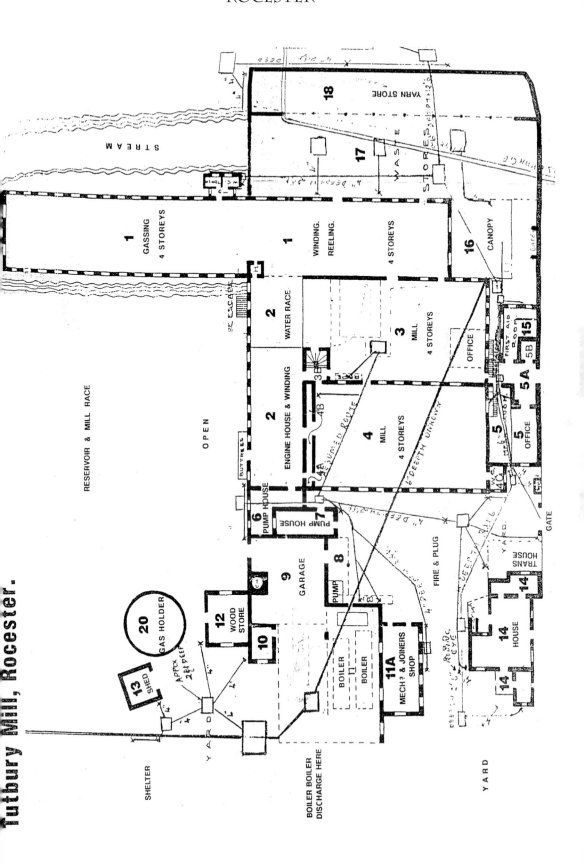

Tutbury Mill, Rocester.

Tutbury Mill. Central
photograph shows the
water race.

The Mill Manager's house.

Mill Foreman's house.

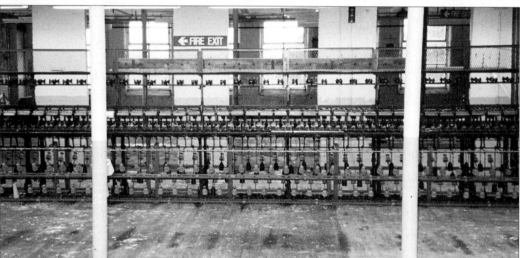

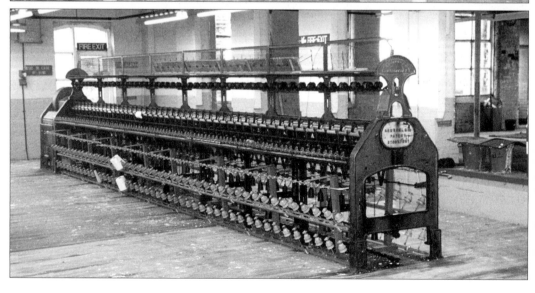

Internal views of the Mill showing the old beams thought to be ships' timbers.

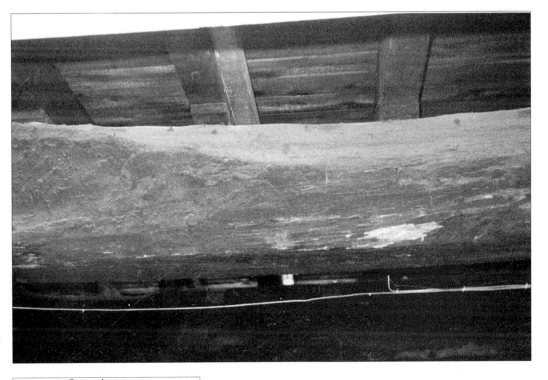

Opposite page:
Further internal views of the Mill.

Internal view and Water Tower
at Tutbury Mill.

did not have the same rapport with his employees as his father. Tradition has it that a dispute between William and the employees reached breaking point and one woman, Anna Brandon, went to Reddish and reported certain malpractices.

Why Reddish is not clear, but the result proved to be disastrous for the village when the mill was closed in 1874. The people of Rocester were largely dependant upon the mill for their livelihood. Up to 400 people were at one time employed in the spinning trade - mainly in spinning, although a small amount of associated work called doubling also took place. An advertisement in the *Uttoxeter New Era*, in 1855, reads:

Doublers and Winders wanted at Rocester Cotton Mills. A few families consisting for the most part of females from 14 years of age and upwards, or single women, will meet with constant employment. Learners will have reasonable assistance while learning the business. Nb Widows with large families will be preferred, and none need apply whose characters are indifferent.

When Rocester mills closed in 1874, it is thought that most of the machinery was bought by the cotton mill at Mayfield, where the Simpsons were cotton doublers. The two years of unemployment that followed would have been hard indeed. Enlightened as the Victorians believed they were, in these decades prior to social reforms and state welfare, an absence of a regular wage caused great hardship.

By 1876 a saviour was at hand. On 3rd July the Lyon brothers, Walter John and Charles William, purchased the mills. The Lyons owned the cotton mills at Tutbury and in their affection for Tutbury the Rocester Mills were renamed Tutbury Mill.* The mills, still used for spinning and doubling, now benefited from considerable investment. It is thought that 170 flyer frames were installed. The old waterwheels were replaced by vertical water turbines built by McAdams of Belfast, at a cost of £5,700. A new wing (Ref. 4 on plan) was also built and a few years later another engine was installed, although this proved unsatisfactory. Steam boilers were added in 1887 and 1889 to replace the ancient pot-type boiler which was withdrawn and used as a tar tank for the small gas producing plant. The gas was used in the factory and in some parts of the village and preceded electricity but it was probably considered a doubtful boon being both smelly and unreliable.

To finance the alterations a mortgage was raised on the property, in May 1878, of £20,000, and was renewed from time to time. On 26th September 1896, shortly after the retirement of Charles William, the mill became a limited company. Walter John Lyon became the main shareholder and William Fearn and John Fearn became a director and company secretary respectively. Why it became a limited company is unknown. Was money required to buy Charles's share? Had finances been over-stretched due to expansion? How much money did the Fearns invest?

Whatever the answers, the decision did not bode well for the future. In 1900 the company went into voluntary liquidation. Initially the company was taken over by Boden & Co., lace manufacturers of Derby and Chard. Perhaps the move was predetermined because on the 13th February 1901 the company Fine Spinners in turn bought them out and took over the six new H & B doubling frames recently installed. Fine Spinners ran the company successfully for many years although they too had their share of disasters.

Towards the 1940s the power problem once again became acute. The installation of a horizontal compound steam engine proved to be a complete shambles. **In 1943 Arkwright's weir, by now under considerable strain, finally collapsed. The turbines were no longer able to function, the steam engines failed and the electricity, installed in 1905, began to malfunction. The company struggled on despite the problems, but breathed a huge sigh of relief when, in 1947, they were able to convert to mains electricity.

For the first time ever a regular source of power was available at the flick of a switch. The gas plant was closed in 1948 and the turbines, known colloquially as Oxford and Cambridge, and Vernon, the main engine, were disposed of. The old order was gone forever. Even the huge fire of 1943 that almost destroyed the mills became a distant memory. Now 20th century post-war technology was preparing for the challenge.

In 1964 the company was acquired by Courtaulds. The original concept of cotton spinning had been in decline since the turn of the century and the list of products sold by Courtaulds illustrate a broad range of textiles. The main product was folded threads of all types made from a variety of fibres. Raw materials supplied by Lancashire Spinners were made into narrow fabrics, sewing threads and knitwear, for sale throughout the British Isles and worldwide.

Courtaulds, a multinational company of repute, ran the company until the mid 1980s when the factory, now old and outdated no longer met the demands of a modern company. Competition for the work force had seen many local people leaving to join J. C. Bamford Ltd - King Cotton could no longer match the wages just across the road.

The closure of Tutbury Mill brought to an end a tradition of industry reaching back over 250 years, and an association with water power on the River Dove and village enterprise that first began over two thousand years ago.

The mills, now semi-derelict, are in the ownership of the Bamford family and used for storage. Surely, one feels, they deserve a more fitting end.

My thanks to Roger Austin whose loan of the records of former mill manager F. Peel proved invaluable.

* Redfern's *History of Uttoxeter* links the Webbs of Clownholme with the Lyons as owners of Tutbury Mill. Although the association is not mentioned by Mr Peel there may be some truth in this - Redfern's book was printed in 1865 so he had first hand knowledge.

** Mr Clark, Trent Catchment Board engineer, noted, when the weir collapsed, traces of an earlier and lower weir. Also when the damn was dredged in August 1950, three lower level sluices were uncovered, the lowest of oak framing, pegged and filled with extremely heavy blocks of stone.

NINE
TRANSPORT AND INDUSTRY

The industrial revolution brought about mass production which, in turn, reduced the price of goods and made them more affordable for the factory working classes. It would, however, have been to no avail without dramatic improvements in transport. Traditionally businesses, large or small, had relied on the packhorse or the horse and cart for the transportation of wares. Both were expensive and slow. They were also limited by the weight they could carry over roads that were rutted and poorly maintained, and by the problems of packaging fragile products. A packhorse, with fully loaded baskets, might conceivably carry several hundredweight and a cart, depending on the size and the number of horses, could manage two or perhaps three tons. In inclement weather business could almost come to a standstill. Trade was often confined to a local area that was within the capacity of the costs, and the strength of man and horse.

Almost on cue for the industrial revolution came, first the canals, and then the railways. Canals had an immediate impact on those within reasonable travelling distance of the wharfs. A narrow boat could carry up to thirty tons, smoothly, consistently and without damage. The costs of canal travel was far below that of the packhorse or the cart, and the businessman was quick to take advantage. There was an explosion in investment in canal companies which gave enormous profits. Canals were cut wherever a profit could be anticipated.

Locally, a Leek millwright, James Brindley, developed such skills in the new navigation that he quickly became a national figure and was in great demand locally and nationally. Brindley was very much the prime mover of the Grand Trunk canal scheme which aimed at linking the River Mersey to the River Trent and providing an east-west waterway between Hull and Liverpool. Branches of the trunk canal would eventually enable towns and villages to link into a national trade route.

One small branch was the Caldon canal which was partly surveyed by Brindley and ran from Etruria to Froghall, a distance of 17 miles. The canal was completed in 1777 and then extended to Uttoxeter in 1811. One of the main beneficiaries was the quarry company at Caldon Lowe. A rail plate way was used to transport limestone from Caldon to Froghall wharf from where it was either shipped in bulk or smelted in the recently built lime kilns. Between 1777 and 1849 four plate ways were laid in a continuing effort to improve the movement of the valuable limestone.

Extending the canal proved equally beneficial to villages en route as well as to Uttoxeter itself. In Rocester the cotton mill found the transport much to its liking as did the brickmaker and the cheesemaker whose premises were but a stone's throw from the wharf.

Local gazetteers of 1793 list the movement of coaches and wagons from

The Railway Station Hotel, Rocester. The hotel was built soon after the Churnet Valley Line was completed in the 1850s. The chimney of Red Hill Bank brickworks is seen hiding behind the hotel.

Red Hill Brickworks, Rocester.

Uttoxeter. The same gazetteer list Rocester's principle businessmen. Cheesemaker and brickmaker are not among them. The gazetteer of 1818 lists Thomas Browne, Cheshire salt, barrow lime, and porter merchant at Uttoxeter wharf. An obvious reference to the canal terminal. Other trades were also becoming established on the banks of the canal. White's gazetteer of 1834 gives Rocester's population as 1,040 and lists a far more extensive range of trades. Now we find the Rocester wharf used by Ford Green Coal Co,. agent John Boulton, Woodhead Coal Co, (and lime burners) agent Anthony Carr, and Joseph Horden, wharfinger and clerk to the canal company.

In White's gazetteer of 1851 we eventually meet the brickmaker, Joseph Horden. Was this the same Joseph Horden who was the canal companies clerk in 1831? Certainly he would have been well versed in the economics of canal transport. The brickmaker occurs frequently, albeit under different names including that of Mr. C. A. Hartley who lived nearby at a large house called The Rookery. Wages during Hartley's time ranged from 3d to 5d per hour for back breaking work digging the rich red clay from the adjacent hillside. By 1932 the brickworks, now quite substantial, was trading as the Red Hill (Staffs) Brick & Tile Co. Ltd. Its decline began about 1938, almost certainly hastened by competition from more efficient companies and the advent of the second world war. The brickwork's finally disappeared altogether when Joseph Bamford purchased the site after the second world war and started the JCB Excavator Company.

Of the cheese company there is no mention although Rocester cheese was well known in the area. This appears to be a strange omission considering that just about anyone from cow keeper to fried fish dealer merits inclusion. Local memory recalls the cheese works in Denstone Lane by Sunnyside Cottage. Denstone Lane has long since been engulfed by the development of JCB. The cheese works, towards the end of its life, was associated with the Great Western and Metropolitan Dairies and later with United Dairies. Prior to its closure in 1926 it served as a milk reception centre.

The fruits of success enjoyed by the canal companies lasted for almost seventy years before the railways emerged and opened up the Country even more with its speedy and efficient transportation. This time the beneficiaries included the general public who were eager to ride in, at first, open carriages, to far flung destinations

The North Staffordshire Railway was formed in April 1845 and one of its projected lines coincided with the route of the Caldon canal. The Canal company was soon taken over by the Railway company, partly through the conditions of the Act of Parliament establishing the Railway. Shortly afterwards the North Rode-Uttoxeter line passing through the Churnet Valley was constructed, opening in 1849. The canal between Froghall and Uttoxeter was filled in and the railway was partly laid on its course. The railways not only competed with the canals but superseded them. Within one hundred years the canals were almost redundant.

The Directory illustrates just how self-contained the township was. The population of 1846 had no fewer than six taverns and three beer houses to provide for the working man. All eight cobblers were kept busy repairing shoes that were expected to last a long time and local shopkeepers had thriving businesses in an age when supermarkets had not been dreamed of. Few farmers actually owned their farms. Just four out of twenty three. Prominent among them is William Atkins, whose descendants still farm in Rocester in 2001. .

No doubt a current gazetteer would highlight the name of Sir Anthony and Lady Bamford, not as residents of Rocester but as principles of the business of JCB Earthmoving. JCB, as it became known nationally and internationally, stands for Joseph Cyril Bamford, the founder and mentor of what became an engineering business of such magnitude that the yellow excavators became a household name and merited inclusion in the Oxford Dictionary. Construction companies did not simply purchase an excavator, they purchased a JCB.

Joe Bamford was a product of a Uttoxeter family that traditionally produced agricultural machinery, the name Bamford being synonymous with reliability and quality. Joe and his brothers Tim and Rupert were destined for the family business where they would, no doubt, have joined an ever growing number of relatives on the board of directors. The management structure was top heavy and family orientated and already stretching its resources, a mistake that Joe never repeated. The management of JCB never became top heavy with family members, although the family always retained full control and total independence of outside financial influences.

Joseph Cyril Bamford was born in 1916 and died in 2001. The son of Cyril Joseph Bamford and his wife Dolores (née Turner) he lived at The Parks, New Road. Uttoxeter. The black and white timber framed house is now a hotel and restaurant, adjacent to the A50. A staunch Catholic, he was educated at Stoneyhurst College in Lancashire from 1927 to 1933 and in 1935 he joined the family firm in Uttoxeter. He was joined there by his brothers Rupert and David (known as Tim). His interest in Bamfords Ltd. was evidently restricted by his own ideas of how the company should be managed, but any thoughts of development became irrelevant when war broke out in 1939.

After the War, with Rupert, Tim and Joe together again, Joe's ambition once again came to the fore. An attempt, almost certainly doomed to failure, was made to take control of the family firm. The resulting dispute put Joe out on a limb. It was possible that the breach could have been healed but for Joe there was to be no turning back. His initial foray alone into the engineering business began in a small lock up garage in Uttoxeter in 1945. From this small building without mains electricity, which he rented for £1.50 per week, he hand built a farm trailer from scrap iron and surplus materials. It took three appearances in Uttoxeter market before the trailer was sold for £90, £45 was in cash and the balance was a farm cart, in part exchange.

Joe was on his way and for the next eighteen months JC Bamford of 28 Derby

The site of JCB factory Rocester c 1950.

Road, Uttoxeter was the only focus of his activity. Until, that is, his landlady, discovering that he worked on Sundays, gave him his marching orders. It was a timely intervention and Joe moved to a larger premises at Crakemarsh Hall where he took over part of a stable block and coach house. This 'larger' factory measured just 60 x 18 feet, but from Crakemarsh a steady flow of trailers saw JCB growing. Joe's biggest problem was a shortage of materials after the War. When he was unable to produce trailers Joe bought and sold ex service jeeps, command cars and army vehicles of all kinds. Joe found that the addition of a 'shooting brake' body onto the almost new road vehicles gave him a much sought after vehicle and a handsome profit. The money was used to good effect. He was a shrewd and innovative engineer and his trailers developed apace. First tipper trailers and then torsion bar independent suspension meant an increasing demand for a JCB trailer.

Joe realised that trailers were still being loaded by hand. So it was, that in 1949 the Major Loader was born. Joe's idea, simple as it now seems, was a major development in hydraulic engineering. The first hydraulic loader in Europe was sold in kit form for £110 and bolted on to Fordson tractors. The kits sold by the thousand and quickly outstretched the capacity of the Crakemarsh factory. By 1950 business was booming and another move became essential. Joe, never short of vision, took a bold step. He moved to Rocester where he took over the remains of the old cheese factory and the adjacent farm land.

Now, with a new factory and room to expand Joe Bamford's inventiveness and engineering ability knew no bounds. In 1951 the Master Loader was introduced and then in 1952 the Si-draulic Loader, the world's first side-mounted loader for tractors. Its high lift and forward reach made it another winner. Shortly afterwards the famous JCB logo first appeared. In 1953 the JCB Mk1 was launched. The Mk1 was, in essence, a Fordson tractor with a front loader and a hydraulic back

Crakemarsh c. 1950, Joe and staff.

hoe. Simplistic but very effective, the secret of JCB success, the principles of the Mk1, remain fundamental to even the most modern of JCB machines.

Over the decades, models were improved. Chaseside Engineering, renowned for its loading shovels was acquired. As a bonus the vehicle registration for Blackburn, the home of Chaseside, was JCB. Joe, never slow to spot an opportunity immediately acquired the JCB series of numbers for use on his company vehicles.

The JCB Mk3, with its ability to operate through 180° took the construction industry by storm. Record sales placed JCB ahead of its competitors. Now the long established practice of hydraulic oil tanks became a thing of the past - the machines were built from hollow section steel work in which the oil was stored.

The new factory was growing yearly and a plan was introduced that would ultimately result in a magnificently landscaped environment complete with lakes that would become home for an ever increasing number of wildfowl. The architect, Brian Carton, designed a factory sympathetic to the Rocester countryside and of such a size that the manufacturing and office facilities covered 110,000 square feet of air-conditioned luxury, complete with theatre, restaurant, design and parts centres.

In later years factories were bought elsewhere. UK, European and world wide dealerships brought JCB to every corner of the world. Expansion into related businesses followed. Tractors of immense power and speed, axles and transmission units built in JCB factories. Recently there has been a new purpose built factory at Cheadle and a World Parts Centre at Uttoxeter, just a few hundred yards away from Joe's childhood home, The Parks.

Joe with son, Anthony, and original employees, 1946.

At the time of writing (2001) JCB is dominant in the small to medium section of the earth moving market in the UK and Europe, and a major player in global terms. To achieve such high standards large sums of money were invested in research and development, around 4% of company sales value per annum.In 1969 Joe was honoured for his services to export when he received the C.B.E. The company has also received many awards.

The success of JCB has drawn a host of important visitors to Rocester including members of the Royal family, Ministers of State and Ministers and dignitaries from overseas. What they see is a factory 'par excellence' - modern, progressive and innovative.

'Joe' Bamford retired in 1976 and his eldest son Anthony took over as Chairman and Managing Director. Anthony, later Sir Anthony, was well versed in the JCB tradition. He was born in 1945 when his father started in business. His mother, Marjorie Griffin, was born in Rocester and retained a long-standing friendship with the children she grew up with. Anthony, very much in the mould of his father, made his own mark and the company continued to grow under his command. Whereas Joe's strength lay in his engineering expertise and his vision, Anthony's lay in corporate management and world marketing. It was the next logical step in the companies progression.

Anthony was educated at St. Bedes, Bishton Hall and at Ampleforth College. After university at Grenoble he took an apprenticeship in engineering with Massey Ferguson at Beauvais in France. He joined JCB in 1965, first in sales and marketing where he helped establish JCB France with Gilbert Johnson. In 1973 he earned the accolade 'Young Exporter of the Year'. He became responsible for all sales, marketing and financial operations prior to becoming chairman and managing director in 1975.

Anthony first married Gillian Shenton who died in a car accident. He later married Carole Gray Whitt of Nottingham. For many years his home was Farley Hall, just a few miles from Wooton Lodge, the former home of Joe and Marjorie. After his retirement Joe had moved to Montreux in Switzerland. Marjorie Bamford remained in England and moved to a purpose built house, Wooton Grange, with her second son Mark. Sir Anthony now lives in Daylesford near Kingham in the Cotswolds, and commutes to the factory by helicopter.

JCB is the largest privately owned company in Britain. The sheer size of it now suggests that it has reached a point where financial rewards are no longer vital. The Bamfords, once humble farming stock, but always resourceful, are now rich beyond compare. Dual nationality and family trusts, vast acres of land and many farms signify great wealth, even before the value of JCB is considered.

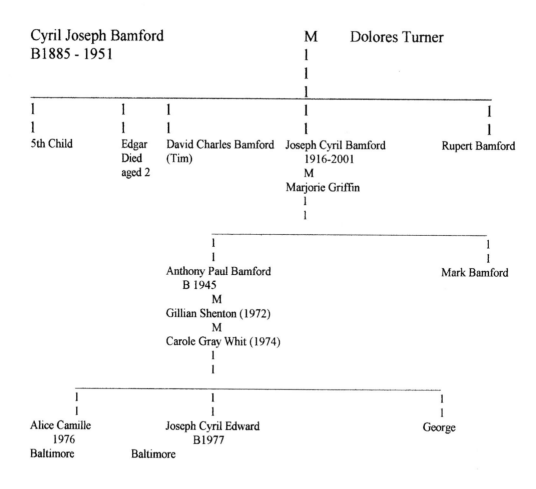

TEN
EDUCATION

Education of village children was limited in the extreme and only began to improve in the late 19th century. All too often a child's education was no better that than of its parents. Many were unable to read and write and, even those considered fortunate to do so, were still poorly educated.

Dame schools were common in rural towns and villages, but such schools could only really be considered as better than nothing. The Dame school was usually run by an elderly lady, sometimes, but not always, with a degree of knowledge in the basic subjects. For a few pence each week a pupil could be taught to read the scriptures, become reasonably efficient in writing and, with luck, gain a fundamental knowledge of simple arithmetic. Any general knowledge gained came from the teacher's personal store of experience. More practical skills such as knitting, sewing and housekeeping for the girls, and gardening and trade skills for the boys, were taught at home. But all too often, children were simply not educated, and were put to work at an early age to supplement the meagre income of the family.

Religion too played its part. The Church of England, and later the Methodist chapels, held Sunday schools each week. Sunday schools were generally well attended by children of all ages and were, for the most part, free. In areas where formal education was limited, the Sunday school was sometimes the only alternative. For the most part they were an improvement on the Dame schools. The teachers were younger, and usually came from a privileged background. The daughter of the squire or the local minister saw it as their mission to help the poor. Any pupils whose aptitude and inclination singled them out as having promise were given extra encouragement and then would become teachers themselves. The extent of the curriculum was again limited to religion, reading, writing and recitation.

The Quakers led the way for a while when they introduced a system to monitor teaching and its rate of success. Even so, without a formal and compulsory system of education the impact was limited.

If a town or village was lucky it would attract the generosity of the wealthy. Money, perhaps from a local person's will, would be given to build a school. It was down to good fortune if a benefactor with a social conscience lived in the area. Rocester benefited from the largesse of the Houldsworth family who owned the cotton mill and employed most of the village. The Houldsworths, mainly Henry, were responsible for building the village school on Ashbourne Road in 1852, although a school was already in existence as can be seen from the Directory of 1834 in which Henry Hollins is listed as schoolmaster and Miss Phillips as schoolmistress. The Rev. Jno Sutcliffe is recorded as a Baptist minister and schoolmaster. The suggestion is that the Ashbourne Road school was built in 1830 and enlarged in 1852. It is recorded that the early school was run with a monitorial

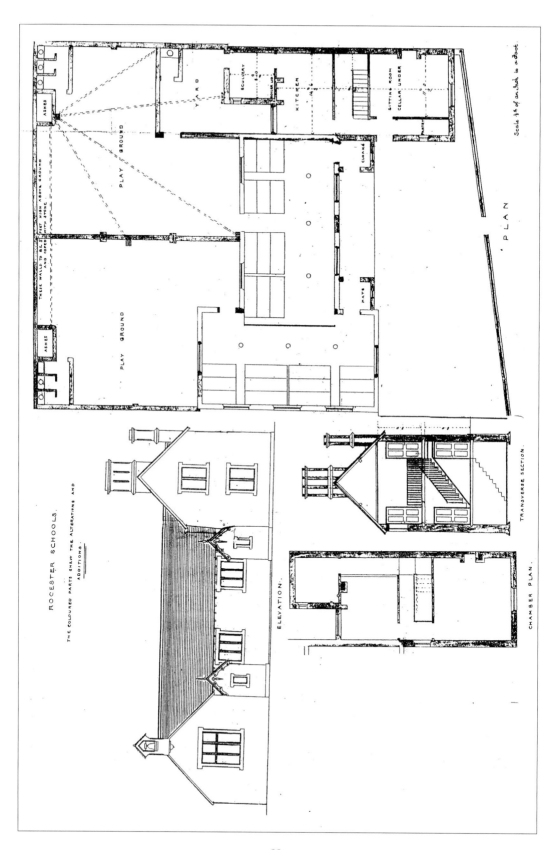

Ashbourne Road school photographs

system wherby the headmaster trained older pupls as monitors who helped to teach the other children.

In 1851 Henry Summers was the schoolmaster and Thomas Houldsworth is recorded as supporting a school for 20 free pupils. The village had over 1,000 residents so a large number of village children still had to find payment or attended Dame or Sunday schools, or simply were not educated at all.

It was a reflection on the social and economic standards of the time and the abscence of the right of the common man, let alone the common woman, to vote in general elections. The National School Board Act of 1870 and the New Elementary Education Act of 1877, were progressive at the time. The details put it into a chilling perspective - among its declarations can be found the following:

No child may go to work under 9 years of age. (After 1877 this is altered to 10)

Children over 9 years of age (except such as have attained the age of 11 before January 1st 1877) may go to work only if they have first attained a certificate, stating that they have passed the Second Standard at School, or that they have attended school 250 times during two previous years.

Every employer of a child not having one of these certificates is liable to a penalty of £2.

If any child above the age of 5 years, and who has no excuse on account of sickness, or on account of there being no school within two miles, is found habitually wandering in idleness, or in the company of bad characters, the Parents of such child, after due warning, may be fined 5/-. And if the Parent still neglects his duty, the fine can be repeated again and again at intervals of two weeks, and finally, if necessary, the child may be sent to an Industrial school, in which the Parent, if judged able, will have to contribute to its support.

Money, very often, was a bone of contention. As education slowly progressed along more formal lines, a school board of managers would attempt to set economic levels of pay and expenses:

Rocester Infants School Annual income for year ending 31st December 1872

	Endowment	Voluntary contributions	School Pence	Totals
INFANTS	None	35 00 00	25 00 00	60 00 00

Number of children 75.   Rates of weekly contributions 2d to 1d

Rates of payment may vary according to the means of the parent but the highest class should be accessible for a fee fairly within the means of a common labourer in the neighbourhood.

The £60-00-00 per annum was used as follows:	£ s d
Salary of teacher	@ £36-00-00
Salary of assistant	@ £ 1-00-00
Books and apparatus	@ £10-00-00
Fuel and lights	@ £10-00-00 *
Repairs	@ £ 5-00-00
Other expenses	@ £ 8-00-00
Total	£60-00-00

*Most schools had a coal fire as the source of heating and oil lamps for light

The site of the Ashbourne Road School built in 1830.
The school here was extended in 1880 to take 220 pupils.

The Dove Lane School built in 1852.

In 1862 a revised code of education had made it compulsory for all schools receiving a government grant to maintain a school log book. As it was an ambition of all schools to obtain finance from any legitimate source, the log book became common throughout the Country. The number of pupils attending also increased dramatically. The Ashbourne Road school housed most of the village children.

A recent picture of Ashbourne Road School - now a private dwelling.

An infants school was also in existence on Dove Lane, not far from the church. The log book retained by the infant school mistress, whilst recording the everyday activities of school life, also highlights the difficulties experienced by teachers. In addition to the four and five year olds, a babies class had to be cared for. Parents appear to have used the school as a nursery rather than an educational establishment. On many occasions babies were returned to their homes because they were dirty and unkempt. The school inspectors had little sympathy. Despite having to look after seventy children, sometimes alone and at best with two unqualified assistants, the schoolmistress was criticised because the babies class was considered backward and in need of extra tuition.

Agnes Slater, who became schoolmistress in 1897, managed to improve the schools performance and also meet the inspector's demands over the development of the babies class. Agnes Slater dedicated herself to Rocester Infants School until illness forced her to retire in 1914. By this time the school had developed a routine which subsequent schoolmistresses were able to build upon.

From the three log books relating to the Infants School we pay tribute to:

1887	Feb.	Miss Elizabeth Cockman	Schoolmistress
1889	April	Miss Charlotte Warren	"
1890	July	Miss Mary Ellen Spare	"
1896		F. M. Brindley	"
1987	Nov.	Agnes Slater	"
1915	June	Mrs. M. Hetherington	"
1918	Jan	Miss Stevens	"
1932		Florence Groutage	"
1934		H. L. Marshall	"
1936	Sept.	Mary Walker	"

After leaving the Infants School the children enrolled at the new 'National School' on Ashbourne Road. The Church continued to play a positive, not to say dominant, role in the running of the school. In addition to the normal curriculum, great emphasis was placed on the catechism. Children found to be deficient in the scriptures were drilled by rote until they were familiar with both the old and new testaments, the psalms, the parables and numerous hymns.

The lot of the head teacher was not made easier by the constant absenteeism of children through illness, poverty and sometimes the need to work on farms or at home. At the first opportunity many children were sent to work at the cotton mill. Assuming, of course, that they had survived the annual bouts of scarlet fever, whooping cough, mumps, influenza, croup, impetigo and ringworm. Death among school children was not uncommon. Croup or influenza was a common diagnosis and such deaths were aided and abetted by poor diet and the absence of adequate medical treatments. Dr Bamford, who was employed by the education authority, often found it necessary to close down the school for several weeks during epidemics.

As might be expected, the winters were a testing time for teacher and pupil alike. The school was heated by a coal boiler which was totally inadequate. Temperatures as low as 40°F made it virtually impossible to teach on some days. Dr Bamford rightly considered that a child was better off at home in front of a warm fire.

The head teachers were stoic to a man. They stuck to their task and slowly but surely gave village children the education their parents had missed. The role of the church was not always appreciated. In 1873 the head teacher, James Abbot, became so frustrated with the interference of the vicar, the Rev. Hunt, that he left the school and took up a similar post in Lincolnshire. If James Abbot was frustrated, imagine the feeling of his predecessor Frederick Jenkins, who lost one of his two pupil teachers because the school could not afford to pay the meagre fees. Sarah Waterall found herself out of a job. It was the same Mr. Jenkins who recorded attendance as thin on the 7th May 1869, the children preferring to visit the Wombells Wild Beast show that had arrived in the village on the previous evening.

Even so, the gradual improvement in education continued. In 1903 the school passed to the control of Staffordshire County Council. Rocester Council School accommodated over 100 pupils. With financial support and the advent of more inspectors, health visitors, hygiene specialists and physical training experts, the welfare of children improved in leaps and bounds. A little later in the 1920s, free school milk came in and then the school canteen and school dinners.

Equally important was the installation of electricity. In October 1934 the gas generated by the cotton mills and used for lighting in the school was discontinued as the plant came to the end of its life. As a temporary measure, oil lamps were reintroduced but, by January 1935, electricity had made a welcome arrival. For the first time the school had adequate light on even the dullest days.

The 1940s saw the arrival of evacuees from Manchester, Ramsgate, London, Croydon, Essex and Leyton. The capacity of the school was tested to the full. Whilst village schools had always coped with large numbers, the need for more schools had long been apparent.

The end of the War brought a determination to introduce radical change. Grammar Schools and Secondary Modern Schools were built to accommodate the extra pupils generated by the extension of the leaving age to fourteen, then fifteen and later sixteen years of age. Rocester Secondary Modern School, built in the 1950s, catered for children between eleven and fifteen years. The

Evacuees arriving at Caverswall

Dove Lane First School.

village school was changed to a Primary School and later, with the advent of the comprehensive education system, the Secondary school, Ryecroft, was classified as a middle school. The Ashbourne Road school, so long the bastion of village education, was approaching the end of its life. Extensions to the newer school on Dove Lane, and a reduction in pupil numbers, finally bought about its demise.

The village school on Dove Lane became Dove First School and catered for children up to the age of nine. The fifty year span between the end of the second world war and the beginning of the 21st century have encompassed dramatic changes in education and living standards, and the welfare and health of pupils.

Dove First School.

Head Teachers of Ashboure Road School

1864	Frederick Joseph Jenkins
1870	James Abbot
1873	Benjamin Wilmott James Haslem
1878	James Gandy - replaced through illness 1909 - resigned 1911
1910	J. William Lowe - temporary
1910	J. Henry Davis
1911	John James Hetherington
1918	Alfred Joseph Jones
1941	G. E. Gibbs
1943	Frank Brereton Alexandra
1962	Eric Wood

ELEVEN
ABBOTSHOLME

Abbotsholme was founded in 1889 and occupied the house that was the original Clownholme. Clownholme, after substantial alterations, became Abbots Clownholme, and finally, with the advent of the school, Abbotsholme.

The school's founder, Cecil Reddie, was raised and educated in Scotland. As a young man he became very interested in the work of Edward Carpenter, Patrick Geddes and John Ruskin. These three intellectuals had long espoused radical Victorian traditions and values and Reddie found their ideals much to his liking.

Reddie met with Carpenter at the latter's home in Millthorpe, near Sheffield, where he outlined his plans for the ideal school. His ideas met with enthusiasm from Carpenter and also Robert Muirhead, a mathematics lecturer who also originated from Scotland. The three developed their plans and began the search for a suitable premises, although Reddie had little money to fund such a venture. Fortunately, a business man from Scotland, William Cassels, had been introduced to Reddie. Cassels agreed to join the venture and provide the finance.

Early in 1889 the search for premises took Reddie to Abbots Clownholme, which was for sale after standing empty for several years. Reddie considered the place ideal and persuaded the others to visit it. Cassels was equally delighted with the estate and moved there at the end of May 1889. Carpenter withdrew from the venture at this point. For the remaining three the die was cast and work on the new school went ahead at a frantic pace. Teachers and staff were appointed, furnishings and equipment purchased, and a school uniform designed. Pupils were even found for the opening on October 1st 1889. The school aims declared:

> The school will be opened on 1st. October 1889 in the Peak District of Derbyshire..... The bracing upland climate and the varied scenery of the Peak Country, the great expanse of wild moors, and the comparative remoteness of the nearest towns, will guarantee to the scholars the health and freedom of a country life, which are so necessary to the young but are now becoming daily harder to secure.

Despite all adversity, it has established itself not only as a familiar part of the village of Rocester, but as part of the educational elite.

Reddie's contribution was not without incident. He had several nervous breakdowns during his time as headmaster, and there was ongoing discontent among staff, at one stage, open rebellion. Even so Reddies contribution cannot be over emphasised. It was he who laid the principles and established the disciplines so vital to success in education. Further headmasters have made important contribution to the developing character of the school.

Cecil Reddie	1889 - 1927	S. D. Snell	1967 - 1981
Colin A Sharp	1927 - 1947	Malcolm Robinson	1981 - 1983
H. C. Humphries	1947 - 1955	Tony Price (Acting Head)	1983 - 1984
Robin Hodgkin	1955 - 1967	Darrell Farrant	1984

TWELVE
CATHOLIC, METHODIST AND PREACHING HOUSE

Henry VIII's wilful destruction of the monasteries and blatant abuse of the Catholic church immediately spawned an underground network of priests and clerics determined to keep faith with long held beliefs. East Staffordshire, with its proximity to Burton, Tutbury, Rocester and Croxden was particularly strong in the catholic faith.

Mary Queen of Scots engendered much support among the local gentry during her imprisonment at Tutbury and Chartley. Even so, opposition to the Church of England required careful planning and subterfuge. The saying of mass was punishable by death or, if you were more fortunate, a large fine or imprisonment. Little wonder that the catholic movement all but disappeared for almost two hundred years. Those that secretly remained true to the

'Catholic' Chartley and Tutbury where not far away.
Here the ruins of Chartley c1900.

faith proved to be the catalyst of revival and benefited accordingly from the degree of tolerance that emerged towards the end of the 18th century. The number of Catholics in the county of Staffordshire is recorded as 3,000 in 1767. A government act in 1712 made catholic chapels legal provided they were registered with the appropriate authority. Thirteen such chapels were opened immediately.

Hoar Cross had a chapel in 1791 and by 1851 catholic chapels could be found locally at Alton, Alton Castle, Cotton, Cheadle and Uttoxeter. Despite the proximity of catholic strongholds in Alton and Uttoxeter, or possibly because of it, Rocester struggled to maintain its own Catholic presence. The wooden hut, situated by the corn mill in the fields by the River Churnet, that served the catholic community, could hardly be called a chapel. No doubt it served its purpose well enough although it must have been with some relief that they moved into the former Methodist chapel on the High Street.

John Wesley, the founder of the Methodist movement, visited Staffordshire in 1738. His timing was perfect. Dissent within the Church of England had reached serious proportions and a simpler and more honest alternative was welcomed by the working classes. The catholic church, still in the act of re-establishing itself was

Wesley preaching in the open, as was his wont.

not seen as an option. Methodism took the County by storm and for over a hundred years chapels were built here, there and everywhere. Country towns, moorland villages and remote hamlets built chapels in support of the movement.

Ironically, just as splits within the hierarchy of the Church of England brought about Methodism, similar splits changed the new movement. Some Methodist ministers, becoming disillusioned with their own sect, sought a return to their radical origins. When changes were not forthcoming, the non-conformist movement split up - and more chapels were created. The New Connexion, Wesleyan Methodists, Primitive Methodists and Congregationalism became prominent in the area.

The Church of England, the Catholic Church, and the non-conformist churches all vied for the attention of the church-goer. Nowadays churchgoing is much reduced and many churches and chapels have closed. Even so some tiny chapels are still attended in the most remote parts of the county.

Local histories and gazetteers record Rev. Sutcliffe as a Baptist Minister and schoolmaster at Rocester in 1834.

The Rev. J. Sutcliffe is again mentioned in 1851 when three chapels are recorded. Baptist, Methodist and Primitive Methodist.

Perhaps of greater interest is the letter sent to Thomas Hill by the registrar of the Diocese of Lichfield.

I do hereby certify that the dwelling house of Thomas Hill and now in his possession situated at Rocester in the county of Staffordshire and Diocese of Lichfield and Coventry (a certificate having been exhibited to the Bishop of Lichfield and Coventry) is registered in the registry of the said Bishop as a place of public worship

Former Methodist Chapel, built in 1837, now Catholic St Joseph's.

for the use of Protestant dissenters according to an act made in the first year of King William and Queen Mary Chapter eighteen entitled "An act for Exempting their Majesties Protestant subjects Dissenting from the Church of England from the penalties of certain laws". As witness my hand this sixth day of August in the year of our Lord One thousand eight hundred and twelve.

Signed
Mm Mors. D. Registrar

The date of 1812 would indicate that Hills House was used as a Baptist meeting place. Other documents in the Stafford archives record the application of Richard Chamberlain of Uttoxeter to erect a chapel in Rocester in 1837 to be used as a place of worship by a congregation of Protestants.

A Primitive Methodist chapel was built in 1888 in place of an older chapel situated on the opposite side of the road. The cost is given as £1,400 and the number of seats as one hundred and fifty.

The Wesleyan chapel built by Richard Chamberlain in 1837 was in a serious state of disrepair by 1889 and an application was made to the Wesleyan Chapel Committee in Manchester to renovate the building completely at a cost of £100. Such was the state of the chapel that the midden heap from the adjacent pig sty was piled against the wall causing great unpleasantness to the congregation.

Repairs were required to the roof, the fabric of the building, ventilation, heating and lighting, and external groundwork. A temporary debt of £31 was agreed and repayments had to be made over 4 years. A loan from Charles Bromley Woolrick of £20 was to be repaid at 4% interest.

The Committee were rigid with their conditions but approval was given for:

1) Repairs to roof, new spouting and drainage.
2) Re seating the chapel, supplying rostrums, stove and flooring.
3) inside and outside painting walls, distempering and erection of coal place.

Costs	£	s	d
Building, drainage, light, heat etc.	70	00	00
Roof etc.	17	00	00
Ventilation	3	00	00
Architect/Clerk of works	5	00	00
Expenses	5	00	00
Total	100	00	00

The money to be obtained from:	£	s	d
Subscriptions and promised	44	00	00
Estimated Public collections	25	00	00
Temporary debt	31	00	00

Cost of local labour	£	s	d
Stanton & Betany - Rebuilding wall and erecting out offices	19	15	00
Thomas Cope - Joiner	1	08	06
Phillips - Plumber	3	08	00
Forrester - Painter	1	00	00
Brain - Blacksmith	 7		06
Total	25	18	06
Rev. T. Law. Promissory note	20	00	00
	45	18	06
Less cash in hand	22	09	01
Present debt	23	09	05
Debt sanctioned	31	00	00

Receipts			
Amount raised by subscription	44	05	11
Collection	49	13	09
Grant/Debt remaining	23	09	05
Total	117	09	01

Estimated annual income is given as:			
Seat rents	3	10	00
Anniversary sermons	5	10	00
Contribution from Sunday School	1	00	00
	10	00	00

Expenditure	£	s	d
Cleaning and lighting	4	00	00
Insurance from fire		3	00
Cost of repairs		6	00
Subscriptions to Chapel Fund		5	00
Incidental expenses		4	06
Surplus re reduction of debt or chapel in connexional purposes	4	18	06
Total	10	00	00

CHAPEL ENLARGEMENT—DEBT.

WESLEYAN CHAPEL COMMITTEE.

CENTRAL BUILDINGS, OLDHAM STREET, MANCHESTER, *2 Octr* 18*89*

DEAR SIR,

The Wesleyan Chapel Committee have considered an Application, signed by yourself and *Messrs William French, Edward P. Parker, J. Payne Hull & Hey Dutton* , for their consent to the *Alteration* of a Chapel

at *Rocester* , in your Circuit, at a cost of £*100* , including Purchase, [or capitalized value,] of Land, Cost of Trust Deeds, Lighting, Warming, Fencing, Architect's Commission, and all other expenses ; and I am now authorized to forward to you their OFFICIAL SANCTION to such *Alteration* , subject to the following conditions :—

1. That except as specified in conditions No. 2 and No. 3, the entire cost on all accounts shall not exceed the sum of £*100 as per schedule.*

2. That should any unforeseen circumstance render it necessary to alter the proposed plans, *so as to increase the expenditure beyond what can be raised in accordance with condition* No. 3, you will request the sanction of the Committee, as directed in the "Compendium of Regulations," inserted in the Minutes of Conference for 1866, Section IV., (IV.) 6.

3. That , the entire liabilities shall be defrayed within twelve months after the re-opening, except £ *31* which shall be paid off within a period of *four* years by equal *annual* instalments of £ *4 : 15 : 0* so as to leave, after such period, NO DEBT on the Trust on account of this *Alteration.*

4. That if additional Land be purchased, it shall be secured to the Connexion according to the provisions of the Trust-Deed of the Chapel ; and that the Trust-Deed for the additional Land shall be duly enrolled in Chancery within six months after the acquisition of the Land ; or, if such enrolment be not legally necessary, that the said Instrument shall be either so enrolled, or sent to the Chapel Committee to be registered.

5. That the Trustees will annually subscribe at least *5/—* to the Wesleyan Chapel Fund.

6. That a reasonable system of Seat-Rents shall be maintained, and the surplus Income appropriated, so far as circumstances will justify, to the support and extension of the work of God in your Circuit, or in aid of our Connexional Institutions.

7. That you will make no definite arrangements as to the *re-opening of the Chapel* until you have obtained the formal consent of the Committee for the purpose.

8. That the Trust-Premises be sufficiently insured against loss by fire.

The Committee request that this Document be inserted in the Trustees' Book, to be preserved as a permanent Record.

I am, dear Sir,

Yours faithfully,

Rev. John W. Henham,
Uttoxeter

H. J. Pope

N.B.—Before giving consent to *re-open the Chapel* the Committee will expect to be assured *that the above conditions will be duly fulfilled, and, if additional land be acquired, they will wish to see the Trust-Deed for its settlement, or a Draft of it.*

[250—VIII.—87—J.B.]

[National Society's Form No. 10]

DIOCESE of *Lichfield*

RURAL DEANERY of *Uttoxeter*

No.

REPORT OF RELIGIOUS INSTRUCTION.

Rocester / SCHOOL.

Infants' DEPARTMENT.

Inspected *June 24th* 189*8*

The Rev W. C. Wright Correspondent.

I. SPECIAL RESULTS OF EXAMINATION IN THE SEVERAL CLASSES AND SUBJECTS.

		DIVISION			
		I.	II.	III.	IV.
	NO. PRESENT	25	42		
Knowledge of	Old Testament *	V. G	G		
	New Testament *	V. G	G		
	Catechism *	V. G	G		
	Prayer Book *	V. G	—		
Repetition of	Scripture *	G	G		
	Hymns, Collects, &c. *	G	G		
	Catechism *	V. G	V. G		
Writing	Abstracts, or Writing from Memory *				

* (V.G.—Very Good. G.—Good.) (V.F.—Very Fair. F.—Fair.) (M.—Moderate. B.—Bad.)

2—GENERAL REPORT.

Considering that Mrs Slater has only been in charge of this Department for 6 months and the Assistant Teacher has just left the School, these children have passed their Examination very creditably. Care should be taken not to press the Scholars to learn too many Texts by heart, and that the answering should be rather more general. Many of the children answered briskly and intelligently but some care in the Upper Division gave no answers at all even to quite easy questions.

Henry R. Oldham

Diocesan Inspector.

THIRTEEN
SPORTS AND PASTIMES

Despite the long hours of work and the limited free time, the people of Rocester have shown a remarkable capacity to organise social and sporting events. The venue for most outdoor activities has centred on the field behind the mill house on the banks of the River Dove. By the end of the 19th century cricket, tennis and football were all popular.

The village football team still enjoys popular support a hundred years later and, although success is limited in the early days of the 21st century, the recent past produced a host of silverware. Precisely when football became the nation's most popular sport depends very much upon interpretation of the rules under which the game was played. There is ample evidence to suggest that youngsters enjoyed kicking a ball about early in the 19th century, whether the ball was a pig's bladder or a bundle of rags.

The sport was obviously growing in popularity by 1843 when the University of Cambridge attempted to standardise the rules. The attempt met with reasonable success and, in turn, encouraged a more formal level of control when the Football Association was formed in 1863. Within a decade, clubs were being invited to play for the FA Cup which originated in 1871.

Enthusiasm for the game was nationwide and friendly matches, formal or informal, were a weekly event amongst towns and villages. The claim by Ian Cruddas of Rocester Football Club is that the club was in existence in 1876 and played on a pitch on Mill Street, opposite the cotton mill.

In 1888 the first formal football league was formed. Stoke City were considered good enough to be among the founder members. Rocester were then playing on a regular basis, and they were the forerunners of a local club that has existed for over 125 years

Early records of Rocester matches are not to hand, but occasional records indicate the teams existence. In 1904 the club was presented with a new strip by the owner of the Red Hill Brickworks. The colours of black and amber were also the racing colours of the horses kept adjacent to the owner's house, The Rookery, which stood at the top of the hill opposite the brickworks. For many years the club was known as Red Hill F. C. although the impetus for its continued existence came from within the village. With the decline of the brickworks in the 1930s the name of Rocester Football Club was adopted.

The club was successful in the first part of the 20th century with honours gained in 1920/21, 1924/25, 1929/30 and 1930/31. The full list of honours illustrates a continuity to be found in very few local clubs. In 1987 the clubs ambitions were matched by a new ground. Financed to a large extent by local business man Don Hill, the new ground, complete with stand, changing rooms and floodlights, met the requirements demanded by the senior leagues to which the club now aspired. The site of the new pitch, behind the cotton mill, was formerly a part of the original area used by the Romans when the township was established. Appropriately, the team became known as The Romans - previously it had enjoyed the name of The Tigers, a name which originated after the second world war when the village policeman was the club chairman, no doubt because of the black and amber strip.

The individuals who run the club are the epitome of village life. Resolute and hopeful they continue to serve both club and village. At the time of writing, the club is experiencing a decline and relegation stares them in the face. But with 125 years behind them the club will no doubt pull up its socks and look to new challenges.

ROCESTER F.C. 1930-1931.

Rocester F. C. Officials 2001

Chairman	Alf Hawksworth	Physio	Mick Ede
Co. Secretary	Ms. T. H. Chell	Bar Steward	Eddie Gregory
Dep. Chairman	Ian Cruddas	Groundsman	Charlie Parkes
Football Secretary	Gilbert Egerton*	Programme Editor	Barry Brosman
Commercial Manager	David Lane	Safety Officer	Ian Cruddas
Team Manager	Martin Smith		

Sponsors Host   Martin Hannibal
Hospitality Hosts   Sandra Ede and Helen Owen
Rocester Juniors Chairman: John Connolly

Directors: A. Hawksworth, T. Chell, G. Egerton, C. Capestake, E. Gregory, C. Parks, P. Cook
Ground: Hillside, Mill Street, Rocester (named after Mr. Don Hill)

*Gilbert Egerton is a long service official of Rocester FC with over 50 years.

Rocester Football Club Honours

1920/21	Uttoxeter & District Amateur League Champions
1924/25	Derbyshire Medal Winners
1930/31	Leek & Moorland Cup Winners
1930/31	Ashbourne News Cup Winners
1952/53	Staffs & District Amateur League Div. III Champions
1954/55	Staffs & District Amateur League Champions
1955/56	Staffs & District Amateur League Champions
1954/55	Staffordshire Borough Cup Winners
1955/56	Staffordshire Borough Cup Winners
1954/55	Staffordshire Pageant Winners
1955/56	Staffordshire Pageant Winners
1957/58	May Bank Winners
1958/59	May Bank Winners
1930/31	Uttoxeter Challenge Cup Winners
1955/56	Uttoxeter Challenge Cup Winners
1958/59	Uttoxeter Challenge Cup Winners
1961/62	Uttoxeter Challenge Cup Winners
1977/78	Uttoxeter Challenge Cup Winners
1970/71	Staffs County League (North) Div.. I Champions
1960/61	Staffs County League (North) Premier Cup Winners
1976/77	Staffs County League (North) Premier Cup Winners
1979/80	Staffs County League (North) Premier Cup Winners
1985/86	Staffordshire Senior League Champions
1986/87	Staffordshire Senior League Champions
1986/87	Staffordshire Senior League Shield Winners
1985/86	Staffordshire F. A. Vase Winners
1987/88	Staffordshire F. A. Vase Winners
1987/88	West Midlands (Regional) League Div., I Cup Winners
1987/88	West Midlands (Regional) League Div.. I Champions
1997/98	Interlink Express Midlands Alliance Runners Up
1998/99	Interlink Express Midlands Alliance Champions
2000/01	Staffordshire Senior Cup Finalists

Horseracing also made a brief appearance in Rocester in the early 1900s but soon succumbed to the more successful meeting at Uttoxeter racecourse.

When an indoor venue was required, events were staged in the 'institute', at the original infants' school on Dove Lane. Mobile film shows appeared in the 1950s and a little later wrestling and boxing attracted large and vocal audiences. Prominent among the boxing fraternity was the gypsy bare knuckle champion, Bartley Gorman from Uttoxeter. Gorman's promotions usually took place in the Victoria Hall in Stoke on Trent, although exhibition bouts were staged at Rocester, involving local champions including Sam Gorman, Bartley's brother.

A most popular activity was the village carnival with its procession of decorated floats led through the village by the local band or the Boy Scouts. In the days before radio and television the village looked inward for its entertainment.

Carnival processions. The Carnival was very strong in the period between the two world wars when their main purpose was to raise money for the local voluntary hospitals.

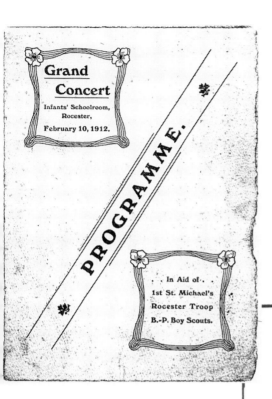

Grand Concert programme 1911.
Inside of programme page 108.

Coronation festivities 1912.
Inside of programme page 109.

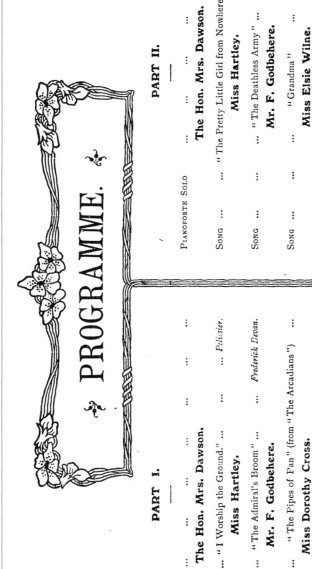

PROGRAMME.

PART I.

PIANOFORTE SOLO	... ...	**The Hon. Mrs. Dawson.**		
SONG ...	... ...	... *Pelissier.*	"I Worship the Ground." ...	**Miss Hartley.**
SONG ...	... ...	*Frederick Bevan.*	"The Admiral's Broom" ...	**Mr. F. Godbehere.**
SONG ...	... ...	...	"The Pipes of Pan" (from "The Arcadians")	**Miss Dorothy Cross.**
VIOLIN SOLO ...	...	*H. Phillips Thomas.*	"Canzonetta"	**Mr. J. C. Burrows.**
SONG ...	... ...	...	"Jammy Face"	**Miss Elsie Wilne.**
SONG ...	... ...	...		**Col. B. C. P. Heywood.**
SONG ...	... ...	*Coleman.*	"Empire Song"	**Boy Scouts.**

Presentation of Troop Flag by Capt. Dawson, the Donor.

PATRIOTIC SONG ...	"Land of Hope and Glory"	**Miss Dorothy Cross.**

PART II.

PIANOFORTE SOLO	... ...	**The Hon. Mrs. Dawson.**		
SONG ...	...	*John Neat.*	"The Pretty Little Girl from Nowhere" ...	**Miss Hartley.**
SONG ...	...	*H. Trotère.*	"The Deathless Army" ...	**Mr. F. Godbehere.**
SONG ...	...	...	"Grandma"	**Miss Elsie Wilne.**
VIOLIN SOLO ...	...	*Rubenstein.*	"Melody in F" ...	**Mr. J. C. Burrows.**
SONG ...	...	...*Pelissier.*	"My Moon" ...	**Miss Dorothy Cross.**
SONG ...	...	...		**Col. B. C. P. Heywood.**
SONG ...	...	*Bonheur.*	"The King's Own" ...	**Boy Scouts.**

GOD SAVE THE KING.

Accompanists:—Hon. Mrs. Dawson, Miss Twigg & Mr. S. Jones.

ORDER OF PROCEEDINGS.

6.0 a.m.—Peal of Bells by Parish Church Bellringers.

9.0 a.m.—Children meet at Schools and march, led by the Rocester Brass Band, to Church.

9.30 a.m.—Children's Service; after which, procession will be made to the Village Square, where their Coronation Song will be sung; then, on to

10.15 a.m.—Receive Memento Mugs, with Milk and buns, generously given and presented by Mr. AND MRS. S. KEELING, of "Riversfield."

11.30 a.m.—Meeting of Parish Councillors, School Managers, Members of Friendly Societies, with their banners and regalia; Residents and Friends, at the Station, whence, headed by the band, a Procession will be made through the Village to the Parish Church for

12.0 noon.—The Special Coronation Service. After Service there will be a Recession as far as the Square, where "Rule Britannia" will be sung, accompanied by the Band.

RULE BRITANNIA.

WHEN Britain first at heaven's command
　Arose from out the azure main,
This was the charter of the land,
　And guardian angels sang this strain,
"Rule Britannia, rule the waves,
　Britons never shall be slaves."

The muses still with freedom found,
　Shall to that happy isle repair,
Blest isle with matchless beauty crowned,
　And manly hearts to guard the fair!
"Rule Britannia, rule the waves,
　Britons never shall be slaves."

ORDER OF PROCEEDINGS.—(Continued).

1.30 p.m.—Lunch in the Large Schools for adults (over 14); each one to bring own knife and fork.

3.30 p.m.—Tea for Children (all under 14), at the Infants' School (if fine at the Vicarage). Afterwards Children's Sports, Music and Dancing, in the field kindly lent by Mr. Atkins.

Tea and Light Refreshments.

NATIONAL ANTHEM.

GOD save our gracious King,
Long live our noble King,
　God save the King.
Send him victorious,
Happy and glorious,
Long to reign over us,
　God save the King.

O Lord our God arise,
Scatter his enemies,
　Make wars to cease.
Keep us from plague and dearth,
Turn Thou our woes to mirth,
And over all the earth
　Let there be peace.

Thy choicest gifts in store,
On him be pleased to pour,
　Long may he reign.
May he defend our laws,
And ever give us cause
To sing, with heart and voice,
　God save the King.

REV. W. C. WRIGHT, Chairman.

S. KEELING, ESQ., Hon. Sec. and Treasurer.

The High Street.

Ashbourne Road.

FOURTEEN
LAW AND ORDER

Almost every town and village had a number of authoritative figures who kept an eye on activities in the vicinity. The Overseer of the Poor and the Village Constable appear on documents over many centuries. It was they, along with the local magistrate and the Lord of the Manor, who maintained law and order. They were also responsible for the overall care of the village, its upkeep, the state of its roads and general well being.

Government changes towards the end of the 19th century and the beginning of the 20th century placed more power in the hands of local people. The parish council was introduced to give an electoral body to govern village affairs and this usurped the role of the overseer.

The constable, so long a local figure of authority, also began to see changes in his work. The demise of the constable who answered only to the local town came at the beginning of the 20th century, with a nationally controlled constabulary and management at county or city level.

This consolidation of the rules of law and order gave a new feeling of security to the population, but the village constable was still very much part of this. Young and old alike respected the village policeman. The 'Bobby' had the good sense to dole out instant, but minimal, punishment for minor offences. A firm warning, a scuff around the ears or a kick up the backside, was enough to keep a youngster out of court. Very often the same punishment was meted out by an angry father after the policeman had lectured him about an errant child.

The old village policeman had certain advantages. He lived in the police house in the village, so he was a permanent presence who knew everyone and was available at all times. Also people did not travel readily and strangers stood out like a sore thumb. Added to this any local malevolents were well-known. Certainly, crimes were committed, but the local policeman usually had a good idea where to look for the culprit.

In the late 1960s and early 1970s two more changes began to take place. Both were to have a dramatic effect on the police force. Alcohol had always contributed to crime but an even greater menace, drugs, especially heroin, exacerbated this. The crime rate soared. Similarly, the detection rate deteriorated. The criminals now had cars and a motorway system. The village policeman was no longer seen as relevant as police cars and general mobility became important.

All these changes are reflected in the memories of the village policeman Byron Davies, born in 1924 and raised in Stoke on Trent:

I was destined to serve the public in one-way or another. While at Longton High School, with six other pupils, I tried to join the army at the age of sixteen. We were unsuccessful but we were allowed to join a unit that trained prisoners for entry into the army. At the age of eighteen I finally achieved my ambition and joined up. Towards the end of my service I was stationed at Barnstable in Devon where I met my wife to be, Joyce Holland. In 1946, we returned to Stoke where I joined the Staffordshire Constabulary, serving at Brierly Hill, West Bromwich and Abbots Bromley before moving to Rocester in 1950.

I remember vividly my arrival at Rocester, and it was the beginning of the happiest time of my life.

I arrived at Rocester, with my wife and family and duly turned up at the new police house on Mill Street. I had the shock of my life. The house was absolutely immaculate. The windows sparkled, the paintwork shone, the floors were cleaned and polished. The ladies of the village, particularly Mrs Fairbanks, Mrs Large and Mrs Webster, had worked long and hard just to make us feel welcome. I was so impressed. From that moment on I knew that this little working village would be an important part of our life. These were ordinary working class people like myself, and they were kind and helpful and a pleasure to be with. Here my son and daughter grew up, both attending the village school, passing the eleven-plus and going on to the local grammar school in Uttoxeter.

For many years I ran the village soccer team. We were very successful. Up to seven or eight busloads of spectators travelled with us to our away games. It was great fun for footballers and spectators alike. The youngsters in the local villages had football and many other activities to engage them. There were problems occasionally, but nothing that could not be sorted out. I was always reluctant to arrest people if I could sort it out informally. Even when the boys from the Reform School at Riverside absconded, they usually ended up at my house. Joyce and I would feed them and take them back to Riverside.

I worked long and unsociable hours. I patrolled the area either on foot or by cycle, in all weathers. I was a part of the village, and the village became part of me. I was very sorry to be transferred in 1965.

Byron Davies was one of the old type 'bobbies', among the last of his breed. He served before the days of political correctness and before parents threatened prosecution if their child was reprimanded for his obvious misdemeanours.

A few years after Byron left, Police Sergeant Jim Capper arrived at Rocester. Jim served at Rocester from 1974 to 1978 and was part of a reorganisation to cope with modern crime. From 1973 Rocester became the centre of a rural police area covering Rocester, Denstone, Ellastone, Mayfields and Marston. Jim, assisted by five officers, patrolled the area by car, and the Rocester station remained open twenty-four hours a day.

Jim's wife became an unpaid assistant in the centre, where police work had now changed completely. The old order was a distant but pleasant memory. Criminals, more sophisticated and highly mobile, made the policeman's lot more and more difficult. Then, ecomomic considerations created a need to reduce manpower - which in turn made the job more difficult.

Even so the people of Rocester remained the same. Jim's memories of Rocester are also mainly pleasant. He recalls:

One night I was roused from my bed at about 2 am by the sound of a persistent, blaring car horn. I quickly dressed and walked into the village where I found three local men in a drunken state making a nuisance of themselves. But a few choice words sent them packing, and next morning, rather sheepishly, they came to collect the car. It was a low-key result to a minor incident that was quickly forgotten by me. A few days later I was called to an incident in the Tattersall bar at the Uttoxeter racecourse. A brawl was in progress as two drunks tried to bat the living daylights out of each other. I had seen this sort of thing many times before and it usually looked far worse than it actually was, although I was a little concerned for the young policewoman who was with me. The fight moved into the toilets and I went in to sort matters out, wondering if I was going to have problems. I need not have worried. The three Rocester lads who I had recently reprimanded appeared by my side. They had been in the bar and saw me facing the brawlers. When the chips were down those Rocester lads were on my side.

One day my daughter Lesley came rushing into the house. "Dad, Dad," she cried. "There's a man in the churchyard who's been killed by Apaches". I knew we lived in the sticks but Apaches seemed a bit unlikely. Even so I raced after Lesley towards the churchyard. I caught up with her as she paused next to a gravestone. There it was in bold letters, ------ APPLETON OF CLOWNHOLME FARM. KILLED BY APACHES. His family at Clownholme obviously brought him back to Rocester for internment!

The Village centre and police station 2003.

The church choir.

A village Carnival procession in recent years in Station Road.

FIFTEEN
ROCESTER MEMORIES

Margaret Clark

I was born in 1915, a few years after my parents had moved to Rocester from Northampton. We lived in Station Road where my father ran his bakery business from our house across from the railway station. He rose at about 6 am every morning to bake the bread and even earlier on Bank Holidays when the demand was greater. Our flour was always 'Spillers' and was supplied by a firm called Cheshires of Derby who sent it to us on the train.

My parents spent their life in our bakery and when they passed away I continued to live there myself, until 1968, a period of fifty-three years altogether. The house and the shop gave me many happy memories. We delivered bread every day to local farms and to houses in Rocester, Denstone, Quickshall, Ellerstone and Marston. We had competition of course, but it was always friendly. We even helped each other when problems occurred. It was a lovely, friendly time. I remember that a two pound loaf cost 4½d in 1949. It was not sliced or wrapped - just freshly baked.

Living near the railway station we often used the train to visit Uttoxeter and Derby. We could even reach London without a change if we used the loop line at Uttoxeter. In the 1930s we could go to Blackpool illuminations for 1/6d.

I remember the first car in Rocester. It was a large black saloon owned by Jack Holmes who kept the Queens Arms. Jack also used the car as

The Clark's shop in Station Road.

a taxi. Sometime later my father purchased his first car, an Austin Seven, from Fryers of Uttoxeter. The garage manager gave him a few instructions and off he went. No one took a driving test in those days.

When I learned to drive, I did take a test, although it was still not compulsory. My first car was also an Austin Seven and my last one, the one that I sold in 2002 when I stopped driving, was a Ford Fiesta. My eyesight was starting to fade but I had done quite well up until then.

There was a milk factory across the road from our shop and, across the field, where JCB is now, was Taylor's Piggery. There was also a cheese factory but I cannot recall the details. The road to the cheese factory was removed when JCB expanded.

By the crossroads, behind the old corn mill, there was a stone yard run by Stanton and Bettaney. The stone came from Hollington and was carried by horse and cart past our house. Hollington stone was used to build Coventry Cathedral after the War and, much of the work was carried out by Stanton and Bettaney. It was said that the work would either make or break them. It was obviously the latter because the stone yard stopped trading shortly afterwards.

Across the road from the corn mill was a row of terraced houses. Churnet Row was known to we children as Tub and Bucket Row because the only water they had was rainwater that was drained from the roof into tubs and then bucketed into the house. There were lots of small shops nearby. Two butchers, a cobblers, a chip shop, a cycle shop, Bindsworth's store and a post office and sorting office.

We could go into Ashbourne or Uttoxeter by buses that did a circular tour of local villages. Slater's of Ashbourne were first in the 1940s and then Bayless Buses followed. I remember Bayless was taken over by Trent Buses.

Many of the village men worked at the brickworks on Red Hill. It was definitely Red Hill - I know because that was where we played in the clay when we were children. When the men were thirsty they could visit the Railway Inn, which was close by. Mr. Jardine was the landlord. The owner of the brickworks had a house at the top of the hill called The Rookery and built with Rocester bricks.

Shirley Glover. Born 1928

My very early years were spent in a small terraced house in Station Road - we lived at the opposite end to Clark's Bakers shop. One of my earliest recollections is seeing my father pumping water from the well. It was beautifully tasting water -no additives present or required.

Shortly afterwards we moved to number seven West View. These houses were built by the owner of Rocester Mill for his employees. There were several rows of such houses in the village, built specifically for that purpose.

I lived close to my best friend Gilbert Egerton and I well remember Gilbert's father Ernald Charles Egerton, who was well known throughout the village. Ernald used to go around the village lighting the gaslights each night. The gas was supplied by the mill and was made from coal that came by rail from Wales. The gas produced was considered quite dirty, but the mill tried hard to improve the quality by introducing various purification procedures. The entire village, including the church, used gas for lighting - in the church now, the candles stand in what was once the gas mantle holder. The gas was made in the gas boiler and was then stored in two huge gasometers next to the mill. At one time many houses in the village were supplied with a small gas stove on which a kettle could be boiled.

Gilbert's father had a second task each day. Each morning Ernald would walk around the village carrying a long pole with a hook on the end of it. He used the pole to hook onto a lever which turned the gas on or off. Every morning, as he turned the gas off, he would stop at the mill workers houses and use his long pole to tap on the bedroom window. This was during the years just before the Second World War. Ernald was probably the last local person to be called the 'knocker upper'. It may seem strange but people could not afford to be late for work and Ernald's persistence was much appreciated.

I started at Dove Road Infants School when I was five. When I was eight I went to the village school on Ashbourne Road and remained there until I was fourteen. The headmaster was Mr Jones and his assistant was Miss Marshall. I think the schoolmistress at the infants was Mrs.Hall, who came from Spath. Being a church school we were visited frequently by the Rev. J. B. Colley who gave us Religious Instruction. This was in addition to the usual subjects of arithmetic, English, history, geography and, of course, gardening, which utilised the school garden. The girls also went once a week to the mill manager's house for cookery lessons.

The school also served as a Sunday school, which I also attended. We used to save a few pennies each week towards our annual Sunday School day trip to Blackpool. We also had day trips from school from time to time and usually went just up the road to Ellastone or the Weaver Hills. We could easily have walked that far, of course. At one time, during the War, we were joined by evacuees from Margate, Manchester and Ramsgate. I remember Norma and Vera Marsh who came from Ash in Kent. There was also the Groombridge family who remained in the area after the war. Joan Webb returned home for a short while and then returned to Rocester. Joan married a local man called Roberts.

When I left school I got a job in the engineers shop at Bamfords in Uttoxeter. My first wage was 2/6d a week (12$\frac{1}{2}$ p) and, after three months, it increased to 5/. As my bus fare to Uttoxeter was 6d return I had nothing left at the end of the week (5 x 6d was 2/6d, half my wage). I quickly found myself another job and, at the age of fifteen, I joined Rocester Mill where I worked in the fitting shop. My wages increased to 19/- per week and I felt like a millionaire.

I was to remain at the mill for forty-eight years until I retired. I became the Works Engineer and was luckier than most people. My job, whether maintaining machinery or installing new plant, was always in demand. This was in sharp contrast to the ladies who ran the machines and some of the men who transported cotton and equipment around the factory.

When sales were falling and work was slack, the mill hands were simply laid off. It was not unusual for them to come to work at seven only to be sent home again at eight because there was no work available. It was then a case of walking to Uttoxeter to visit the dole office that was housed in an upstairs room, next to Orme's Furniture Store in the Market Place. The shortage of work was not made any better by the pressure put on the management to employ displaced people from Italy and Lithuania after the war.

The hours could be long at times and I often worked twelve hours a day. The mill ran on two shifts. One was from 6 am until 2 pm and the other from 2 pm until 11 pm. For the morning shift I had to go in early to start up the machinery which meant starting at 5 am and finishing at 5.30 pm. I think people generally worked harder then.

I remember when Rocester Mill was purchased by the Lyon family from Tutbury. Initially workers came in from Tutbury across the fields. They arrived on Monday, stayed *all week and went home at the weekend.*

Ladies in the village would also work from home on small spinning machines in order to eke out the family income. One lady I knew, Lucy Mansfield, started to work before she finished school. She would go to school from 6 am until 12 noon and then go to work in the mill in the afternoon. The pattern was reversed the following week. Lucy left school at thirteen. I have a photograph of Lucy when she was Mrs Coxon. She married Jonathon (Jonty) Coxon. Jonty was an ex army man who had served in India. During the First World War he was employed to train recruits before they went to the front. Jonty swore he was simply training young men to be killed. Afterwards he became the Rocester postman. The mail was sorted at the old post office on the High Street before being delivered by Jonty. He walked his round twice a day between Rocester and Croxton. Some years later he had the privilege of a cycle - and all for a wage of 10/- a week - but the cycle would have been much appreciated. Cars were few and far between - the Doctor had one and also the mill owner but not many other people.

The austerity of the Second World War continued until the 1950s. We had to be self-sufficient. Every house had a large well-kept garden, we fished, caught rabbits and generally survived as best we could. I do remember when the weir water was flushed through the sluices, large numbers of eels were left floundering on the grating by the water wheels. One man at the mill used to grab them and hang them on a hook. He then skinned and salted them ready for slicing up and cooking. Even after they were dead, the eel steaks used to jump about in the frying pan. The nerves seemed to respond for ages.

Food and clothes rationing remained in force for several years. When I married Joan (Basnett) in November 1949 we were only allowed to have thirty guests because of the food restrictions. We married at Rocester and held the reception in the Haddon Room above Elkes café that stood on the corner of Uttoxeter High Street and Carter Street. Elkes made

Extreme left, Jonty Coxon. Extreme right, Lucy Coxon (Nee Mansfield).

the cake and we just about had enough food coupons to provide for our thirty guests with a ham salad lunch with trifle to follow.

The bride's and bridesmaids' dresses were made locally and I had just enough clothing coupons left to buy myself a made to measure suit from McKnight's of Hanley. After we were married we moved to number 11 West View.

Ken Langton. Born Rocester 1936

My grandfather was Edmond Langton who ran a grocery store and bakery on the High Street. My father, also Edmond, helped in the shop from an early age. He used to relate stories of how he delivered bread to Denstone on Saturday mornings for a wage of just one penny (1d). It was inevitable that I should continue to run the shop and remain in a local business all of my life. I even remained in the same house.

Trades change of course, just as circumstances and demands change. My father started to trade in cycles in the early 1900s. Cycling was in its infancy and cycles were in great demand. My father repaired cycles as well as selling them, both new and second hand.

During the First World War my father served in the Royal Flying Corps in France. The flying machines included a basic engine that turned a wooden propeller by means of a bicycle chain. My father's expertise as a cycle mechanic meant he was in great demand. This, of course, was in the days before the R.A.F. was formed. My father died when I was seventeen and I took over the cycle business with my mother's help.

By the 1960s the golden age of cycling was on the wane. Cars and buses meant travelling was easier that way - the cycle trade was bound to diminish. I changed the business to suit demand and gradually moved into electrical goods such as radios, televisions, washing machines etc. Even so business was changing all the time. Supermarkets and multiples drew people to the towns and village trade suffered. My own

Rocester c. 1900.

business survived well enough even though the village was changing all the time. At one time there were twenty shops and four pubs, The Cross Keys, The Railway, The Red Lion and the Queens. Now you can count the number of businesses on one hand.

In 1981 the opportunity arose for me to take on the Post Office. When I became sub-postmaster I also began to sell stationary, pens, magazines and associated products. Another part of our shop sold toys. I was probably at the end of an era. I ran our village shop until I retired on 10th July 2002.

I remember also a little bit about my mother's father, my granddad Collins. He came from Hampshire and was employed as a fishing and water bailiff by Sir Percival Heywood at Doveleys. Sir Percy was very wealthy and had fishing rights on the River Dove that ran through his property. Grandfather lived in a cottage on the estate by Barrow Hill.

Sir Percival gave considerable amounts of money towards the building of a school, a church and a vicarage in Denstone where he was considered to be the local squire. He also contributed towards the building of Denstone college.

The local roadman was Charlie Harrison from Churnet Row. Other characters were Raggy Jack from Churnet Lane and Old Annie, a domestic who worked for Dr Hill on Mill Street. Dr Hill visited his patients on horseback. I recall the schoolteachers, Miss Swinson and Miss Brookshaw, at the infants and Mr Alexander and Mrs Taylor at the Ashbourne Road School.

We had film shows at the school - silent movies through a 9.5 mm projector operated by a master from Abbotsholme School. The Youth Club, started in the late 1940s, fared a little better with a 16mm projector and a real sound track! For the real cinema we went to Uttoxeter. The Queens Cinema was, as the name implies, on Queens Street. On the way into town we had the Elite Cinema, which was built, in the grounds of Uttoxeter Manor. Both cinemas were owned by Mrs Stebings who lived in either Ashbourne or Derby. Going to the cinema cost 9d plus the bus fare from Rocester - we went on Trent buses for 4d return.

The brickworks had more or less closed when I was a boy. The Rookery, formally the home of the boss of the brickworks, was then occupied by Mr Simister who was a corn merchant. Corn used to arrive at Rocester station and was stored in the old canal warehouse, which stood where the JCB social club now stands.

Paul Harrison

I was born in 1951 and brought home to the Lodge at Barrow Hill Hall. My parents had lived there since they got married because my father was Head Gardener and my mother was in service at the hall. I can't remember when it was that Dad stopped working for the Dawson's at the Hall because I was too young, but he began to rent the walled garden at the rear of the Hall and ran it as a market garden business with his brothers. 'Harrison Bros' continued to trade until Dad retired in the 1970s.

Some of my earliest recollections are of conditions that would not be put up with these days. No electricity, no running water, no mains sewers. Dad brought drinking water down from the gardens each evening. This was from a spring at Quickshill, just outside Denstone, which ran into a man made well and was pumped to a holding tank under the highest point of Barrow Hill. It was then piped through the gardens to Home Farm and the Hall. Dad and Bill Grindy from Home Farm took it in turns to check the level in the holding tank and when necessary they went and primed and started the motor that drove the pump to fill the tank. They normally took a gallon of petrol with them - it was run until the petrol ran out and the pump would stop. I remember being told to go to the top of the hill and listen if the motor was still running. The drive belts were always breaking and Dad and Bill had to repair them. (I don't know for sure but I think this job may have been part of their rent agreement).

Water for washing our clothes and ourselves was collected rainwater from the roof. It was channelled into a tank and we had a manual pump in the kitchen over the sink. The loo was outside the back of the house next to the coalhouse. As we had no sewer and no septic tank, facilities were VERY basic. The toilet had to be emptied, and the sewage buried in a deep hole in the garden at regular intervals.

On washday, we had a copper in the kitchen under which we lit a fire to heat the water. Everyday hot water for washing ourselves and for the dish washing came from the boiler at the side of the fire range in the sitting room. As far as I can recollect it wasn't until around 1960 that we were connected to the mains water supply. For the luxury of a 'proper bath' I had to visit a relative's house.

Light was supplied by candles and paraffin 'tilly' lamps, until we had gas mantles powered by calor gas. Cooking was also done by calor gas. We used torches for night trips to the loo, because when it was windy the candles would get blown out. I also remember going to a neighbour's house by torchlight to watch their new television. Our only 'home entertainment system' was a Bush radio powered by an accumulator which had to be taken regularly to Laurie Bowd's garage in Rocester to be recharged.

Each room had a coal fireplace but most didn't get used very often. The kitchen would be warmer on washday, the living room always had a fire but the bedroom fires were only lit if someone was ill. These things may have been improved and modernised earlier than they were, had my Mother been alive, but she had died when I was very young.

Each week I was set a number of tasks to help around the garden, pricking out, cleaning pots, weeding, dependent on the season. These had to be done, along with any homework I had from school, before I could call my time my own. My sister had her own jobs too but these were in the house.

I went to Rocester Infants School in Church Lane. When I was at home Dad took me to school in the van but sometimes I stayed with relatives in Northfield Avenue; it was an easy walk from there. I remember being taught by Mrs Brookfield (Brookshaw?). I stayed for school dinners in the canteen next door to the school, I can't remember what the food was like but I'm sure there was always plenty of cabbage, probably supplied by my Dad's market garden.

As I got older I moved on to Dove County Junior School, Ashbourne Road. Mr Alexander was the Headmaster and he lived in the house next door to the school. There were allotments at the back of the school, on one of which we were given gardening lessons - just what I needed! The only thing I really remember enjoying was playing football. I enjoyed that because it was easy to kick the ball out of the playground into Keeling's Yard and no one wanted to fetch it back because it was where the undertaker made the coffins.

After school we would buy our ha'penny chews and blackjacks from Bob Wood's (I later bought my ciggies from him unknown to my dad - 5 'Domino' in a little square pack, 9d I think) and then congregate in Bull's entry, opposite the Queens Arms Pub. I don't think I learnt much here and consequently I failed the 11 plus and went on to 'Rocester College of Knowledge' - also known as Springfield Secondary Modern.

The Headmaster at the time was Mr Hudson, known to us all as 'shush' because he hated to hear anyone talking in the corridors or classrooms. Academically I must have improved a little here. With a little help from my friends I ended up as head prefect. I enjoyed sport, especially football, and a few years later I got a place in the team at Rocester FC, sometimes playing in the County League and other times in the Leek and Moorland League. The Manager, who had the inspiration to succeed, at that time was Ken Green who later took Rocester to the Doc Marten's League.

I remember the tradesmen calling each week. Bill Ratcliffe, the milkman, ran his business from outbuildings of the Railway Hotel, now JCB gatehouse. He drove a three-wheel van - not a normal Reliant - which did not have a steering wheel but had a control like a tram. George Brown, know as wee Georgie Brown because of his lack of height and build, delivered Dad's newspaper. He also brought him his 'Digger Flake' tobacco for his pipe and the occasional small tin of snuff. George's brother, Arthur Brown, ran the Coal Merchants from the station. Next door to this was Simister's Corn Merchants. The Co op van came round on a Friday. This large van was laid out like a shop inside. Holgate's was another mobile shop that came round on a Wednesday. These shops were used by many of the local farming people. Another caller was a man on a bike who used his bike to drive a grinding wheel to sharpen knives etc.

Frank Beteny's fish and chip shop was a popular local amenity although it was only open for a few hours around teatime and then only on two or three evenings a week.

Rocester Station.

Norbury Bridge.

High Street.

Rocester Boy Scouts c. 1950.

The Cotton Mill.

Crakemarsh Hall.

The Old Vicarage.

John Walker, from *Hawkers Galore, Memories of a Uttoxeter Baker*, 1996

Every Friday morning we did a bread and cake round in Rocester village. Starting at Churnet bridge we worked our way through the village to be at the 'Mill' for twelve o'clock. Everyone turned out of the Mill for their dinner hour, and it was a very hectic time supplying the women, knowing that they were all in a hurry to get home! Arkwright's Cotton Mill was the major employer in the area until the JCB factory and the building is now owned by the JCB factory.

John Walker

My Grandma's was one of the last calls in Rocester, the last house of a terrace of twenty four. Every two houses had a shared back yard and most of the space was taken up by a big water tub at each house. My Grandma's was a 72 gallon wooden barrel standing on bricks and covered with a wooden lid amongst other things to keep the light out which turned the water a green cast. One day a vehicle was trying to turn round when it hit Grandma's water tub. The owners of the vehicle replaced it after some time but although she had water 'on tap', rainwater was always used for washing and bathing. This lovely soft water was without equal and Grandma soon pronounced her verdict on washing with tap water. "It's that hard it fair makes your fingers whistle!"

Despite the reasonable prosperity of Rocester, sanitation had not advanced a great deal. Older houses and farms still had earth closets, generally built down the garden and enhanced with a lilac bush or an elder tree. The contents would be dug out annually, in Spring, and tipped into a trench in the garden. This would be the site of the kidney bean row!

Most of the later 'mill' houses had a lavatory with a galvanised iron bucket which was emptied by a man who came once a week. This type of lavatory was often referred to as the 'janker'. The army slang was derived from this word - going 'on jankers' originally meant emptying these buckets as

John's parents, bakers of Uttoxeter. This section is a short and condensed extract from the Rocester chapter of John's book of memories.

punishment. The man who emptied these buckets in Rocester came with a horse and a high-sided cart known as 'the Brandy Wagon'. He was called variously the mixen man, miskin man or the muck man! The women slammed their doors shut, to help keep out the smell as he emptied the buckets into his cart. Often the buckets would be very full and he would inevitably spill some on the ground. He would immediately get the sharp edge of the womens' tongues, shouting from within the house!

When the miskin man finished at Rocester, it was time for his dinner break. The horse would be told to 'stand', the full cart now leaking at the corners where the 'brandy' ran from it in thin streams. The man would sit down on some grassy clods with his back to the fence, take his cap off and wipe his hands on it, before getting his lunch bag out and enjoying his sandwiches!

Friday didn't seem to be an ideal day for taking bread and cakes round! Pedley's bone wagon also called at the butchers' shops in Rocester on Friday mornings. This open wagon collected all the unwanted waste meat, skins, offal, feet and hides. The smell was atrocious, and made the brandy wagon seem like a flower shop by comparison.

After finishing in the village I would call on a few of my old relatives who lived there. First of all I would go to the 'Boot Shop' and see my Uncle Joe and Uncle Amos who would be mending shoes in the 'back shop'. Uncle Amos's crippled daughter also lived here with them. She was struck with paralysis at the age of eleven whilst a boarder at Leek High School. Grace had apparently got out of bed in the night and was struck down and spent the rest of her life in a wheelchair. She was a most happy and pleasant person, always laughing but she had leg irons and it took her four hours to get up and dressed each morning.

Uncle Joe and Uncle Amos were my Grandad's younger brothers. Joe was born in 1870 and Amos in 1867. These old men could not only repair boots and shoes, they also made them, just as did their father, Joseph Forrester, my Great Grandad. The old workshop was a museum in itself - just as it was a century before. Great Grandad's empty seat was still there. On the whitewashed brick walls were religious scripts in frames and Victorian admonitions such as "Cleanliness is next to godliness." There were cricketing invitations (Uncle Joe was a wicket keeper and played his last match when he was 70!) and rows of tools inserted in lines of leather loops. On one wall there were a lot of pairs of wooden 'lasts', each pair for a particular person. There were one or two odd lasts and Uncle Joe said these were for men with a wooden leg. I didn't know whether he was joking or not!

Looking down on the scene was a picture of Great Grandad, white fuzzy beard and sidewhiskers with a clay pipe and a black beret on his head. The little iron stove was kept going with discarded leather soles and heals. All the rainwater from the workshop roof ran into a huge stone cistern in the back yard where sides of leather would be kept soaking.

Uncle Amos died in his eighties, but Uncle Joe kept working until he was ninety. To watch this old craftsman work was an education in itself. You may think that the strong cobblers thread, used for sewing the leather soles, was bought on reels! No such thing - it was made! Uncle Joe would pull a handful of white stuff out of a cupboard by his seat, like cotton wool. Using both hands he would deftly twist and roll it a few times on his apron, and it would become a long white thread. Russian hemp he said it was. This thread was passed round a small nail in a bench about two feet away, keeping it tight. This double thread was then waxed together - it was now strong enough to hold a horse.

Every Friday, as we had a cup of Camp coffee together, he would tell me some interesting facet of his life or of the local history. Uncle Joe told me that his mother and father, my great grandmother and great grandfather, remembered Queen Victoria's accession to the throne in 1837. His father was born in the reign of King William IV and his mother, four years older, in the reign of King George IV. They had nine children, eight boys and one girl. Every dinner-time during the summer they had rhubarb - either in a pie, stewed or in a boiled pudding - and always eaten first to fill them up. Meat, which was expensive, would be the second part of the meal and was boiled in a big pot on the fire, the vegetables cooked with it. The potatoes which didn't require so long were put in a net and dropped in later! From the youngest child to the eldest was a span of thirty years. His mother was also a midwife for the village and the local district. She must have been busy!

In August 1912, his parents had been married for 60 years. In those days nobody had any money so there was no fancy cake or expensive presents, just a few friends and neighbours went in for a cup of tea. Grandma and Grandad were retired from the Boot Shop and lived at 42 High Street, Rocester. Uncle Joe took his Dad two or three bottles of beer and his Mother a few handkerchiefs. You walked straight into the living room off the pavement. Uncle Joe said, "They never saw or heard me. They were kneeling down on the rug in front of the fire, holding hands and saying their prayers."

Uncle Joe said that, in the late 1800s, tobacco firms decided to try and find out who were their biggest users of tobacco. Shops were asked to take note of their best customers and how much they smoked. He said that in the whole of Staffordshire the contest had been narrowed down to two men; his Dad and Mr Twemlow who was the surveyor of Leek. He said that his Dad smoked two ounces of light shag a day and Mr Twemlow came second at one and a half ounces a day!

The taking of snuff was always a big concern at Rocester - with being a mill town - smoking at work was not allowed, so of course snuff assumed the role as tranquilliser! The shops in Rocester not only sold snuff in tin boxes but also loose, then was weighed out into a small paper bag. Some customers would take their own snuff boxes.

In Rocester in the 1890s - my Grandad on the left.